A FUTURE FOR
CHEETAHS

Dr. Laurie Marker

Photography by Suzi Eszterhas

A FUTURE FOR CHEETAHS

Published by Cheetah Conservation Fund
PO Box 2496 Alexandria, VA 22301

Design and Production by Lisa Eng-Lodge, Electra Design Group

Printed and Binding by Friesens Corporation in Canada on FSC-Certified Paper using vegetable based inks

ISBN 978-0-615-93320-7

Table of Contents

Acknowledgements

I have been racing with the cheetah for over thirty years now and
there have been so many wonderful people along the way who have
helped me fight the plight of this iconic species. In particular I would like
to thank our research collaborators, the farming community of Namibia,
and the Ministry of Environment and Tourism for helping us see the
stabilization of the cheetah population in Namibia. I would like to also
thank our Cheetah Conservation Fund's Board of Directors and
Trustees globally for helping us develop an organization to provide a
future for the cheetah and our USA and Namibian staff, our donors,
interns, and volunteers of the Cheetah Conservation Fund
for helping us continue to learn so much about the cheetah.

I would like to give special appreciation for help with this book
to my close cheetah friends Dr. Bruce Brewer, Casey Lay,
Eli Walker, and Patricia Tricorache in editing, Shannon Sharp
and Beth Fellenstein in distribution, and Paula Martin, Laurie Payne,
and Liz Georges in promotion. I want to thank Suzi Eszterhas for
her photographic eye and dedication to help save wildlife through her
beautiful photography and Lisa Eng-Lodge for her great sense of design
and production assistance from the Electra Design Group, Ltd.

We hope you have been inspired to join us as a member of our
Cheetah Conservation Army! Together we can Save the Cheetah.

Dr. Laurie Marker – February 2014

Foreword

George B. Schaller, Panthera and Wildlife Conservation Society

My wife, two small sons, and I spent over three years in Tanzania's Serengeti National Park during the late 1960s. I had come to study the impact of lion predation on the great herds of wildebeest, zebra, and Thomson gazelles. But I was often distracted by the elegant, long-limbed grace of a cheetah scanning the plains for a meal. If I waited, I could usually observe the cheetah tensely stalking a gazelle and then explode with a burst of energy, its body coiling and uncoiling as it accelerated, becoming almost airborne, bounding in pursuit of its fleet prey. A forepaw flashed, the tripped gazelle crashing in a cloud of dust. Each such elemental scene left me exhilarated and with a treasured memory. To learn more about such hunts, we watched a mother cheetah with two small cubs from dawn to dusk – a time when most hunts take place – for 26 days. She killed a gazelle nearly every day, and also one hare. A lion stole the kill twice and a spotted hyena once, a reminder that a cheetah leads a fragile existence in spite of its glorious speed. Other research in the Serengeti followed ours and has now continued for half a century, adding greatly to knowledge.

Without good science, conservation is blind. A basic challenge is how to apply the information to achieve conservation, to actually protect a species and its habitat. The ever-growing human population with its relentless quest for resources is reaching the biological limits of our earth. The cheetah has already been exterminated in 25 of the 44 countries in which it once existed. Shot, trapped, its habitat converted to fields, and natural prey decimated, the species is gone from Asia, except for one known population of less than 100 animals in Iran. As Laurie Marker notes in *A Future for Cheetahs*, about 90% of the estimated 10,000 cheetahs in the wild live outside of protected areas.

What can be done to save the species from slipping quietly away? An appeal to the emotions – to beauty, ethics, and conscience – is one way to reach the public, especially given that fifty percent of the world population is now urban, divorced from nature. To peruse the superb photographs in this book by Susi Eszterhas, looking into the inscrutable amber eyes of an adult cheetah, or admiring small cubs dressed in their silky and silvery mantle of hair, is to behold visions glowing with life.

Yet more must be done on behalf of the cheetah, much more. Research such as mine in the Serengeti does nothing directly for conservation. It takes a Laurie Marker to lead us onto the correct path. For nearly a quarter century her Cheetah Conservation Fund, based in Namibia, has been developing an innovative and highly successful conservation program. We must all learn from it. But to succeed, it takes enthusiasm and dedication, someone with infectious passion, as I note whenever I meet her. It also requires decades of commitment to provide a cheetah population with ecological security.

Laurie and her Namibian team count cheetah numbers, conduct anti-poaching patrols, raise orphan cubs and try to stop the illegal trade in them, to name just four. But even greater involvement is essential. Laurie knows that conservation ultimately depends on the interest in and participation of communities. She reaches out to them and devises economic incentives so that they can improve their quality of life and then also strive to protect land and wildlife. After all, cheetahs occasionally kill livestock.

The establishment of conservancies, in which communities manage their own area responsibly and sustainably and derive benefits, such as from tourism and even from limited trophy hunting of common species, is one approach. Other imaginative economic schemes initiated by Laurie provide guard dogs to protect livestock, establish a goat creamery, and turn unwanted brush into fuel logs to save trees from being felled and converted to charcoal. Also critical are conservation clubs to raise awareness and change attitudes. Their motto is "We can live together".

In 1948, the ruler of a princely state in central India shot a band of three male cheetahs from his vehicle while driving a forest road at night – the last definite record of the species in the country. Let not such vandalism be repeated elsewhere. The fate of the cheetah is in our hands. Laurie has helped to assure this cat a future in Namibia which now harbors one-third of the world's wild cheetah. Every country needs someone like Laurie with the devotion, wisdom, knowledge, and skills, someone to assure this natural treasure, this icon of the savannas, its survival. All who read *A Future for Cheetahs* will be rewarded with deep insight into the species, the challenges it faces, and a feeling of urgency to help it. And there is the insistent message that nature must be treated with responsibility and compassion.

Yes, we must all live together. We must all accept moral responsibility not only for saving the cheetah and its landscape but also all living beings on this small planet.

A Cheetah's Eyes

The cheetah, the world's fastest land animal, is also one of nature's icons. Most people are captivated by their eyes... large and amber, almost mystical. When a cheetah looks at you, it looks beyond you. A quick glimpse has the power to penetrate into your soul and transport you into a different world: a world of past... and future. For the cheetah, their future is unknown and in our hands as humans to ensure they survive.

The cheetah's vision has a depth that is greater than most species. They scan the horizon looking for prey or other predators. It is the eyes of the cheetah that fascinate most people. Beyond these amazing eyes are entire ecosystems, which the cheetah helps maintain through its selective hunting technique which includes spotting prey, stealthfully stalking, and bursting into a short high speed pursuit to make a kill. A cheetah's kill not only feeds the cheetah but other species as well, from jackals and vultures to smaller carnivores and insects. Cheetahs are nature's doctors providing for other species which allows for a healthier ecosystem. If a cheetah helps feed jackals, the jackals don't need to find food in a local farmer's livestock kraal.

The cheetah's eyes are only one aspect of its distinctive physiology. Built for speed, the cheetah is one of the most unique of all species on the earth. Reaching speeds of up to 70 mph, every aspect of the cheetah is finely tuned to allow for maximum precision on the African plains. Scanning the horizon, the cheetah's eyes are shaped in such a way that they can pick up movement from great distances. The cheetah can see up to a mile with as clear a vision as humans can when using binoculars.

Imagine what it takes for a cheetah to find and succeed in making a kill. This unique predator is the pinnacle of perfection. With each stride the cheetah covers 20 feet with just one foot touching the ground at a time; at two points in the stride they are flying through the air with no feet touching the ground. When they are outstretched un-attached shoulder blades and hip girdles allow for maximum extension. Its flexible spine acts like a spring as it doubles up with feet under it to clench the earth with powerful non-retractable claws acting like cleats in the ground, to thrust it into unimaginable speed and maximum distance.

LIFECYCLE

There are three stages in the lifecycle of the cheetah: a cub's life, adolescence, and adult life.

Birth – A litter is born, what will their future be?

After a 93 day gestation, a female cheetah hides herself in thick bush to nest and give birth. Up to six cubs are born (although a very few litters of up to eight have been recorded, these are rare). Alone, she nurses her smoky-grey newborn cubs and rests after the silent birthing. At birth, the tiny cubs weigh about 8.5 to 15 ounces and are blind and helpless. They will live in a secluded nest for the next six to eight weeks, being moved by the female regularly from nest to nest to avoid predators. A female cheetah patiently grooms her cubs, purring quietly to them, providing warmth and security. After a day or so, the female must leave the cubs to hunt for herself, so that she can care for her cubs. This is the most vulnerable time for her cubs, as they are unprotected. The cheetah female is on her own, caring for her cubs for the next year and a half.

▲ At twelve days of age, these cubs' eyes have just opened. At this age cubs have very limited vision and their eyes are very opaque. They can see and track movement but are not able to fully focus on objects.

◀ At five days of age, a cheetah cub's eyes are still closed, leaving them vulnerable when the female leaves the nest to hunt for herself. Although cheetah moms are very attentive to their cubs, she must leave the nest to hunt to keep up her strength. When the cubs are at this age, it is critical that she find prey within no more than a couple miles of the nest.

Even with eyes closed at six days of age, the cubs are mobile ▶ and keep the female busy. In this instance, one of the cubs has crawled out of the nest and the mother is bringing it back. To keep the nest clean and prevent the development of scents that might attract other predators, a female cheetah moves her cubs to a new nest regularly. This mother will soon be making her first move and she moves them by carrying each cub gently in her mouth.

14

The Nest – The mother is the source of nutrition and warmth.

During these first three months cub mortality is highest.
Less than 1 in 10 survive during this time.

Growing Up –
Leaving the Nest

At about six weeks of age, the cubs begin following their mother on her daily travels as she is looking for prey. During these first few months she cannot move far or fast and cub mortality is highest; less than 1 in 10 survive during this time, as they perish from predation by other large predators, like lions and hyenas, or even due to injuries. This is the time when life skills are taught. Playtime appears to be constant, but as they play, they are developing their motor skills, coordination, and learning about the speed and agility of their body. They sit alongside their mother, looking into the veld, as she searches for the next hunting opportunity while on constant vigilance, looking out for predators which could harm her vulnerable, naïve family. There is so much to teach for the cubs to learn life in the wild, for a cheetah has many dangers and challenges.

At six to eight weeks of age, the cubs are able to follow their mom and watch the hunt. Their long mantle hair on their backs may protect them from other predators through mimicry as they possibly resemble the very aggressive ratel (honey badger). Females' ranges are very small during this time. If possible they only travel one or two miles from the nest to find prey. When successful in a kill the female will call her cubs, which are usually left under the protection of a tree or bush, with high pitched chirps inviting them to visit the kill. However, their deciduous (baby) teeth are very small and they are not able to open the carcass; therefore, the female opens it up for them while they become familiar with the kill.

◀ The young cubs lay low as their mother finds food.

This single mother has to catch enough food for her and her cubs to survive the harsh environment.

At two months of age the cubs soon learn how to feed on the carcass and, like their mother, they gorge themselves. Their mother continues to nurse the cubs for a couple of weeks longer but soon they are satisfied with the prey that their mother provides for them. After feeding, mother and cubs sleep. Being diurnal, they are only active early morning and in the cooler late afternoons.

20

Under the Watchful Eyes of Mom

Female cheetahs raise their cubs on their own and are constantly vigilant with a watchful eye for the dangers of the bush: mainly other predators or even baboons. The female cheetah is everything to the cubs; she feeds them, grooms them, and shows them what to watch. At the same time, she is always on the lookout for prey and dangers, while the playful cubs climb on her. Ah, the life of a female cheetah.

Communication is very important among cheetahs. Cheetahs purr during grooming between a mother and cubs, siblings, and coalition males. They are the only big cat that purrs and does not roar; their vocalizations are varied and unusual. They have a dog like bark and a bird like chirp for calling between each other. Other vocalizations include a bubble or "uhun" sound, a hiss, and a growl.

Cubs soon learn that it is important to keep a watchful eye in the
same direction as their mom is looking. Although they often don't
understand why her stare is fixed and don't always see what she is
looking at. Cubs' vision develops over the first few months of their
life. Their lives will be spent looking out for threats and opportunities.

Exploration and playtime. Cubs spend much of their waking hours playing, chasing after each other, and developing their bodies. However, they are always on guard and prepared to flee if necessary.

The Start of the Learning Process

Stalking is instinctual and the small cubs begin to develop their skills: often chasing but rarely catching. At about four months of age, the cubs' mantle is receding on their back forming a long mane. They are more attentive and are able to focus while attempting to follow their mother's line of sight or gaze.

The black blotches behind the ears are obvious to the rest of the cheetah family and are used in subtle communications.

▲ Growing cubs need to learn so many life skills including how to recognize dangers in their environment. Playful experimentation is one way to learn. By poking at it and trying to chase it, this cub will discover that while this tortoise poses no threat, he can't eat it and it does not run. He will soon move on to more amusing educational opportunities!

◄ Between four and six months of age, cheetah cubs are very active and playful. Trees provide good observation points and allow for development of skills in balancing. The cubs' semi non-retractable claws are sharper at this age and help them to grip the trees as they play.

In East Africa, cheetah cubs use tall trees to play in. In Namibia, these trees are called "playtrees." The word "playtree" originated from Namibian farmers naming certain trees as they would come upon cheetah cubs playing on them; this term is now widely used. Today, farmers also call it the "newspaper tree" as male cheetahs use these trees for leaving their scent-marks. Older cheetahs would not be able to go into trees like these, as they are too narrow and steep and do not provide enough space to stand and observe. Learning to climb into trees is also dangerous, as cheetahs have fragile and lightweight bones. Playing in trees like this can be detrimental, as cubs could break bones.

At around eight months old, this cheetah is no longer a cub but has at least another year before it will be independent. The next several months of learning will be the most crucial to developing its life skills.

The Trial and Error of Hunting – The Classroom of the Bush

Learning how to hunt is the most critical survival skill that the cubs must develop. At a year of age they are participating in hunts and the mother, while assuring enough kills for the family's survival, will allow the cubs to develop their skills. They have a few more months remaining of critical development until they will be on their own. The hunt has several components. It includes prey detection, stalking, the chase, tripping (or prey capture), and killing through the suffocation bite. The bush classroom is vast and finding prey becomes the first challenge. Following the mothers gaze to recognize prey is the beginning. Stalking and the chase are the next steps. Their months of play have fine tuned their chase, and then learning the most important part of the hunt is tripping their prey. Coming upon a fawn that perhaps does not flee and bring about the chase presents a new challenge. How do they trip if there is no chase? First they try to get the fawn to move by pestering it or batting at it with their paw. Once on the move, they extend a front paw to trip the fawn. Once down the cubs complete the kill and share the rewards, while the mother continues to watch vigilantly for dangers.

Adolescent – Still Dependent, "Super Mom" on Alert

A mother knows best. Although close to adult size, these adolescent cubs still depend on their mother who's diligence has kept them healthy, making her one of the "super moms" of the African savanna.

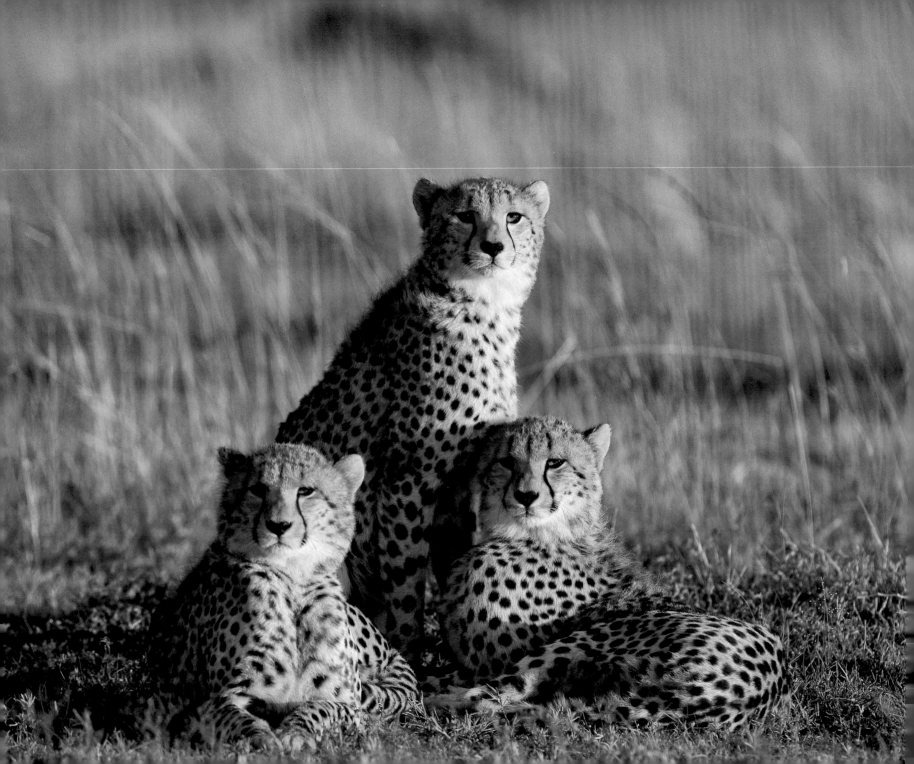

Growing Up – Coalitions

Although not fully adept at hunting on their own, the independent male and female cubs stick together for a few more months working together to master their hunting skills. When the young females begin cycling, dominant males will court them and drive the brothers away. The brothers become dispersal males, on the move for the next couple of years, until they are able to find and defend a territory. They will cover hundreds of miles, being moved out of one area into another, pushed by more dominant males. The young brothers will stick together the rest of their lives forming a male coalition.

The lifelong sibling bonds increase hunting success and defense against predators. They will finally find a place where they can settle.

Adult living is hard. Cheetahs live fast and die young. There is competition between territorial males which often results in death. The lifespan of an adult male is eight years. Adult mortality is one of the most significant limiting factors for cheetah population growth and survival. In addition to territoriality from other male cheetahs, competition with large predators and farmers, poaching, and loss of habitat and prey are factors contributing to early death.

Breeding – Tactics for the Long-Term Survival of the Cheetah

◀ Males will check if a female is in heat by sniffing the ground and trying to get close to the female. Female cheetahs behave in a submissive way, usually chirping loudly. Male vocalizations are a bubble like chirp and a uhun, uhun. If the female is not ready for breeding she will slap the ground, growl, and hiss, at the males pursuing her. Courtship and breeding usually occurs fast, staying together no more than a day or two.

In captive studies, females are known to come into their first estrus around 16 months of age but don't usually breed until they are about two and a half years of age. In Namibia and Botswana females have mate choice and within a coalition only one male will usually do the breeding. However, in Tanzania, females have been found to have cubs produced from multiple mates in one litter. The importance of breeding is about passing on family genes. To the coalition, it is important to have a successful mating. As they are brothers, it does not matter which one of them is successful.

Cheetahs are considered more social than most other felids, with the exception of the lion. In Namibia and East Africa, large groups of cheetahs (up to 19 individuals of different age groups) have been observed, often at waterholes. It is hypothesized that these groups consists of female relatives. CCF's research has shown that female cubs stay within the females' home range in a matriarchal society. In Namibia, females have shown to have mate choice and will travel some distance to go back to the same area to mate. The large home range of a female will cover multiple males' territories, with her cubs getting to know the habitat, visiting "playtrees" and "meeting" other cheetahs along the way. When cheetahs that know each other meet, there is often a chirp followed by a purr, sniffing, licking, and cheek rubbing.

SPEED, ADAPTATIONS,
AND HABITATS

Cheetahs are built for speed with all parts of their body having evolved for precision.

The cheetah is the enigma of the African bush and the best hunter of the savanna. How cheetahs run is often misconstrued to think that these cats, although fast, only run in near straight lines. Cheetahs are built for speed with all parts of their body having evolved for precision. From their small, aerodynamic head, lean body, and long legs, to a flexible backbone and ruder-like tail, allowing for a graceful acrobatics, they are the fastest land animals. Their lithe and flexible body is built to change direction in a split second at the speed of a race car and can run at up to 70 mph while turning 180 degrees. Cheetahs are adaptable and have uniquely evolved with these special adaptation for the niche they fill. They are nature's doctor and feed the whole veld: jackals, vultures, porcupines and beetles.

Cheetahs are found in different ecological regions and thought to have multiple sub-species. Today genetic research has shown that they are all very similar, sharing the same genetic code leaving them more vulnerable to ecological and environmental changes.

Although the cheetah is a survivor, today it has been pushed to the edge; their habitats are fragmented, and more and more people and their livestock are on their land. With competition for the grassland, there are also fewer numbers of wild prey species throughout their range. To survive, they have adapted to areas that have become thicker with bush due to overgrazing and removal of large grazing animals.

Today, cheetahs are living in a human dominated landscape. As habitats get smaller, cheetahs are overlapping more with humans and their livestock. Today, in two-thirds of their remaining range cheetah numbers are so small that these populations may not be viable. There is no wild left; where can the cheetah live in the future?

In Namibia, conservancies are the future. Conservancies practice integrated systems allowing people, livestock, wildlife, and predators to live together.

◀ Small antelope like this fast Thomson's gazelle are the cheetah's main prey, but they have been known also to prey on larger species, especially when an individual is young, old, weak or sick. The cheetah hunts in short, fast sprints and so over the millennia its body has evolved to be aerodynamic, built for speed and precision hunting in every detail.

56

A cheetah's distance vision is as good as a human with an average pair of binoculars. Like all predators, cheetahs make use of cover when stalking, but when locating prey, any elevated mound, rock or tree is useful.

A stalking cheetah is very intent when beginning a chase. All parts of its body are poised and ready for the fast speed sprint. The black tear marks running down from the cheetah's eyes to the corners of its mouth help it keep focused on the prey while it is chasing. The tear marks are called malar stripes and act like a scope on a gun of a hunter. They are also thought to help refract the suns glare.

The Art of Hunting

Successful hunters not only need speed but also stealth. Since cheetahs are only able to chase their prey a few hundred yards, they must get close to their selected prey before beginning their chase. They are like hunters everywhere: moving slow and low in the grass, staying downwind, sometimes using small mounds to see and disguise their approach, and using camouflage to blend in to their surroundings. Antelope, their main prey, are on constant watch for any danger.

◀ Searching for prey, the cheetah gazes the horizon, its main instinct is to always look for possible prey or threats. Their keen eye sight is key to their survival.

Cheetahs hunt in the early morning and early evening. They capture their prey by stalking to within 10 to 30 yards of their prey or as far as 80 yards before beginning the chase. A chase lasts about 20 seconds and rarely longer than one minute. Only 10 percent of their chases are successful. Antelope and gazelles, hare and the young of larger antelope like wildebeest, kudu, or oryx and small warthog often fall prey to the lightning fast cheetahs. Coalition males will often take larger prey like zebra or ostrich. They can accelerate from 0 to 45 miles per hour in two seconds. A cheetah will abort a hunt if the prey dodges and darts from it more than three or four times. Factors that lead to a successful hunt include herd size, prey response, number of cheetahs hunting, and the distance the cheetah has to run. Cheetahs specialize in catching their prey on the move. The cheetah's speed and agility make it the best hunter on the savanna; however, its lack of endurance and its timid nature impede its hunting success. After a fast sprint, the cheetah usually finds shade to catch its breath, as it may need to flee again in case of danger. A cheetah can go days without water because they get the hydration they need from the blood in their prey. Cheetahs gorge themselves on a big enough kill and can fast two to five days; however, they will hunt daily if possible.

Successful hunters not only need speed but also stealth.

Sometimes, large prey stands its ground, and the cheetah is helpless and responds to this threat by growling, hissing, spitting, and foot stomping. The prey will often charge the cheetah in response to this behavior and the cheetah usually then flees.

Running –
The Speed
of the Cheetah

During the short bursts of
speed in pursuit of prey, the
cheetahs' body temperature
elevates quickly. After a
chase, cheetahs need to rest
for up to a half an hour.

To facilitate the explosive
use of energy, the cheetah is
endowed with a physiology
developed so the cheetah does
not overheat. Although the
nasal cavity is enlarged, as
are the lungs, powerful heart,
strong arteries and adrenals,
the heavy rapid breathing after
a chase indicates an enormous
expenditure of energy and
a large oxygen debt. During
a sprint, the cheetah's body
temperature has been measured
at 105° F, or 4° F higher than
their normal temperature.

For increased intake of air, the enlarged nasal passages may have crowded the roots of the cheetah's
canine teeth, thus the reason for their smaller size relative to the teeth of other felids.

During a hunt, cheetahs usually catch their prey after an average 200-yard sprint. Although fast, their ability to accelerate at a high speed is most critical, and their maneuverability to turn rapidly is more important than just their speed. Most hunts take place at a slower speed, as the prey they are hunting is dodging to flee from their pursuer. Cheetahs can accelerate and change directions faster than any other land animal.

The cheetah is the only cat with short, blunt claws, lacking skin sheaths making the claws semi non-retractable thus providing added traction like a sprinter's cleats. The foot has additional adaptations, including less rounded paws than the other cats and hard digital and metacarpal pads that are pointed in the front, possibly to assist with fast braking in sharp turns. Their pads have two ridges that may serve functionally as anti-skid devices, similar to tire treads. Sharp dewclaws on the insides of their lower legs are used like thumbs to hook, trip, and hold down their prey.

The cheetah's long, flat, muscular tail acts as a stabilizer or rudder for balance to counteract its body weight so that it does not roll over and spin out in quick, fast turns during a high speed chase.

◀ Far left:
These six month old cubs, who are just learning to hunt, stand by as their mother prepares to take a pass at some Thomson's gazelles. Even with their precision hunting skills, hunting can be a matter of trial and error. Cheetahs usually only keep their kills about 50% of the time.

Because a cheetah lacks the powerful jaws and bulk of other big cats, it kills prey with a combination of precision and speed. After a short, fast sprint, cheetahs trip their prey and grab it in a strangulation hold called a throat bite. The prey then dies from suffocation.

Teeth, But Not Aggressive

The cheetah is not actually considered an aggressive animal. When agitated or distressed, they have a low moaning sound. When showing aggression, they will lower their head to shoulder level and growl. Its only form of defense is hissing and showing its teeth, along with spitting and hitting the ground with its front feet. Cheetahs have what is known as a flight and fight distance. If the hissing and spitting do not chase off their adversary, then they will use their only real defense: running away.

Between cheetahs, a fight consists of slapping each other on top of the head with their paws/claws and then trying to bite each other on the legs. In a territorial fight, they will go for the throat in a strangulation hold.

Cheetahs have evolved for speed versus power and aggression. Their bodies are lightweight in comparison to the build of other cats. Their jaws are not as powerful as those of lions or leopards. The cheetah is often mistaken for a leopard. However, the leopard's teeth are nearly twice as long as a cheetah's teeth, and leopards do not run away; they are very dangerous. The distinguishing tear marks of a cheetah on each side of the nose also differentiate the cheetah from the leopard, and the cheetah's coat is tan, or buff colored, with smaller black spots, unlike the leopard, which has what are called rosettes: yellow spots surrounded by black circles.

Other Predators are a Threat

Cheetahs are always on the lookout as the prevalence of predators in protected areas can be dangerous for them. This is one of the main reasons why 90 percent of the remaining wild cheetahs are found living outside of protected lands, alongside human communities. In protected game reserves cheetahs often lose their kill to larger and more aggressive predators. In the Masai Mara, hyenas are numerous and often come into contact with cheetahs. One hyena may be chased off by a hissing angry cheetah, but if there is a kill to defend the cheetah invariably loses.

"Playtrees" – The Newspaper of the Bush

When farmers catch live cheetahs, they often do so at certain trees they call "playtrees" or "newspaper trees." Cheetahs have a very strong drive to go to these trees which serve as powerful focal points in the cheetah's range. These trees tend to be tall with sloping trunks and large horizontal limbs that the cheetah can easily run up into and observe their surroundings from. They leave their scat on the limbs and urine on the trunks as markers. Our research has shown that cheetahs go from tree to tree in their circuitous range. Although several groups of male cheetahs might mark on the same tree, there is a strong avoidance instinct, and subordinate males will move rapidly from the area if a dominant male or coalition of males has left a recent scent mark. Not all farms have playtrees, and we term these farms 'pass-through farms,' as the cheetahs move quickly through on their way to the next playtree. Some farms have several playtrees, others just one. There is a correlation between higher game numbers and the occurrence of playtrees on the farms. Playtrees can be used for tourism, showing visitors a playtree and showing how important the trees are for communication, often finding scat or spoor.

RESEARCH, GENETICS, AND THE FUTURE

Research, Genetics, and the Future

Carnivores have been a strong influence on human lifestyles for centuries through predation on livestock. However, their beauty, intelligence, and enigmatic behavior have garnered our human curiosity to investigate carnivore species' evolution, biology, and ecology and the consequences for them of living in today's human-dominated landscape.

Through in-depth research studies of cheetahs since the early 1980s, today we probably know more about this species than most other cat species and yet the cheetah's survival is still in question.

A potentially critical factor for the long-term survival of the cheetah is its lack of genetic variation relative to other felids. The unique genetic profile of the cheetah species demands a thorough understanding of their biology and capacity for reproduction.

Genetic homogeneity can make a species more susceptible to ecological and environmental changes to which the world is subjected now and has been interpreted in the context of

two potential risks: the expression of recessive deleterious alleles and increased vulnerability to viral and parasitic epizootics that can affect genetically uniform populations. Given the lack of genetic diversity, monitoring the overall health of cheetah populations is an important component of understanding and promoting long-term viability for the species.

At the Cheetah Conservation Fund (CCF), biomedical research is conducted to monitor the wild cheetah population's genetics and health. Captured cheetahs are systematically sampled (blood, tissue, and sperm) and collected for a Genome Resource Bank (GRB) program that can then provide important materials for both the captive and wild population in long-term biomedical research. Nearly 1,000 cheetahs have been sampled and screened since 1991 at CCF's Research Center in Namibia.

Genetic information, accompanied with ecological and ecosystem research, provides direction in developing management strategies and setting priorities for cheetah conservation throughout their range.

Evolutionary History

The cheetah is considered one of the earliest divergences in felid evolution and evolved from the ancestors of other modern Felidae species in North America during the Miocene (~5 million years ago) and then migrated a few million years later to Asia and Africa.[1] Recent research has placed the last common ancestor of all existing populations, *Acinonyx pardinensis*, much larger than the modern species, as living during the Pleistocene (~ 4 to 5 million years ago). More recent fossil finds, such as the *Acinonyx pardinensis* fossils in Asia, are refining this scenario as we are beginning to trace the migrations of the earliest cheetahs across Asia to Europe and, Africa.

Various genera of now extinct cheetah-like species were found in North America and although some were called the "North American cheetah" they are not true cheetahs but close relatives to the mountain lion or cougar. The modern cheetah, *Acinonyx jubatus*, evolved into its present form about 200,000 years ago.

The First of Three Severe Population Declines

Genetic research shows that today's cheetah populations are descendants of but a few animals that survived 12,000 years ago after the Pleistocene era. The population then experienced a founder event, referred to as a population bottleneck. Cheetah populations were widespread in North America until the large mammal extinction event during the Pleistocene era.

Dr. Stephen O'Brien on Cheetah Genetics

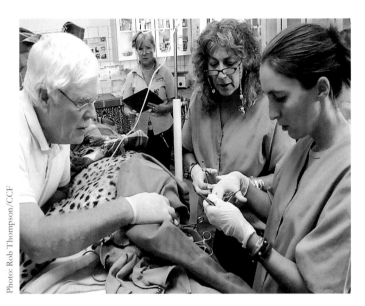

Photo: Rob Thompson/CCF

In 2013, the whole genome sequence of a living cheetah was determined by researchers in hope of reading an unabridged text of the life script that makes a cheetah. The CCF flagship ambassador cheetah Chewbaaka's genome was sequenced from DNA collected by Drs. O'Brien, Schmidt-Küntzel and me, via a small blood sample. Chewbaaka's genome sequence is being mined to uncover the evolutionary secret behind the cheetahs' amazing speed, agility, and survival. This information will be treasured and perhaps employed in the important quest to conserve wild cheetah populations forever.

Led by Dr. Stephen O'Brien and his collaborators, including myself, over three decades several aspects of cheetah molecular genetics have been thoroughly studied and have been the focus of much attention. Phylo-genetic research has shown that the cheetah evolved from a common ancestor with the puma and jaguarondi, in North America, during the Miocene (5 to 8 million years ago) and predecessors of modern day cheetahs were once distributed across North America and Europe. However, by the end of the last glacial period (around 12,000 years ago), the cheetahs had disappeared from most of its prior distribution. Surviving cheetah populations today, display reduced genetic diversity compared to other felids or mammals for that matter, as the consequence of a historic demographic bottleneck that significantly reduced genetic variation. The new polymorphic alleles observed in the populations today have developed by new mutations during the elapsed interval.[2]

The Second Population Decline – Loved to Extinction

The earliest record of the cheetah's long association with humans dates back to the Sumerians in 3,000 BC where a leashed cheetah, with what appears to be a hood on its head, is depicted on an official seal. In Egyptian history it was believed that the cheetah would swiftly carry away the Pharaoh's spirit to the afterlife, and symbols of cheetahs have been found on many statues and paintings in royal tombs.

During his 49-year reign as an Indian Mogul in the 16th century, Akbar the Great had more than 39,000 cheetahs for coursing. They were called "Khasa" or the "Imperial Cheetahs." All these cheetahs were taken out of the wild from free-ranging populations. The Mogul kept detailed records of them which indicate that of all these cheetahs during all these years only one litter was born.

Because of this continuous drain on the wild populations, the numbers of cheetahs declined throughout Asia. They were loved to extinction.

In the early 1900s, India began to import cheetahs from Africa for hunting purposes.

84

HUNTING WITH THE CHEETAH.

Museum of the Baroda Maharaja

In Hindu, cheetahs are called "Chita" or the "Spotted One" and are known as the hunting leopard and the most easily tamed of the big cats.

Cheetahs were used for hunting in Libya during the reign of the pharaohs. Cheetahs were not used to obtain food but for the challenge of a hunting sport known as coursing. In Italy, cheetahs were coursed during the fifth century. Russian princes hunted with cheetahs in the 11th and 12th centuries, and, at the same time, crusaders saw cheetahs being used to hunt gazelles in Syria and Palestine. The best records of cheetahs having been kept by royalty, from Europe to China, are from the 14th, 15th and 16th centuries. Cheetahs also were used for hunting in Russia, and in the 18th and 19th centuries the cheetah rivaled dogs in popularity as hunting companions.

Photo: Museum of the Baroda Maharaja

Adult cheetahs were caught in the wild as they already had well-developed hunting skills; they were then tamed and trained within a few weeks. Cheetahs had several "keepers" who cared for them.

Many of the Maharajahs would take large hunting parties out to watch the cheetahs hunt. The best hunters were revered.

In Africa, the cheetah was important to many local ethnic groups: the San hunting communities of southern Africa ate cheetah meat for speed; traditional healers used cheetah foot bones for fleet-footedness; and kings wore cheetah skins for dignity. These practices, combined with exportation to other countries, also contributed to the cheetah's decline in Africa.

The Third Population Decline – Habitat Loss and Fragmentation

The cheetah was once one of the most widely distributed of all land animals. Through the course of time the cheetah migrated over land bridges from North America into China, through Asia, India, Europe, and finally to Africa, settling in its range as recently as 20,000 years ago.

In 1900, approximately 100,000 cheetahs were found in at least 44 countries throughout Africa and Asia. Today, the current free-ranging populations of cheetahs are found in small, fragmented areas spread in perhaps 23 African countries of North Africa, the Sahel, East Africa and southern Africa, and it is estimated that around 10,000 animals remain, representing a decline of 90 percent over the century. There are less than 100 cheetahs in Iran, the last of the Asian population.

Although seven subspecies were originally proposed based on morphological criteria, five subspecies are currently considered valid by most taxonomists.[3] Today, viable populations may be found in less than half of the countries where cheetahs still exist.

All populations of cheetahs are listed on the Convention on International Trade in Endangered Species of Fauna and Flora (CITES) Appendix I and are classified as Vulnerable or Endangered by the International Union for Conservation of Nature (IUCN).

Cheetahs Throughout their Range

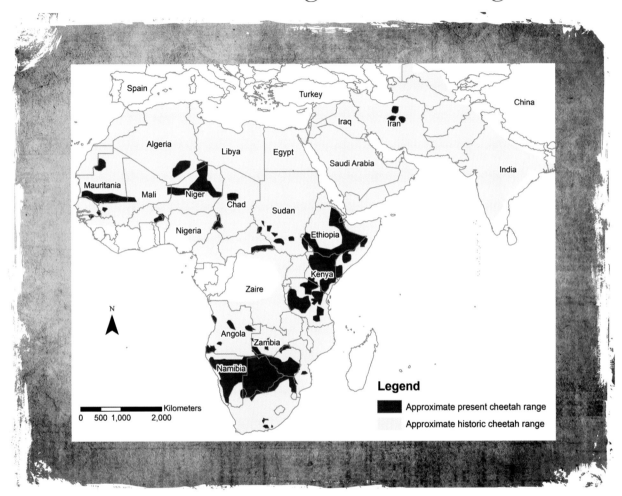

Legend

■ Approximate present cheetah range

　Approximate historic cheetah range

All cheetah populations are threatened due to habitat reduction and decreased prey, resulting in human/livestock conflict issues. An evaluation of conservation priorities in order to understand the issues for the future of the species in each country is underway. The remaining strongholds for cheetah are Namibia, Botswana, and Zimbabwe in southern Africa, and Kenya and Tanzania in East Africa.

Research – We can learn about biology but we need habitat as there's no place to go.

Photo: Eli Walker/CCF

I founded CCF in 1990 and based our International Field Research and Education Center in Otjiwarongo, Namibia where the highest concentrations of wild cheetahs are found. Here we set the standard for cheetah research everywhere. Visitors from around the world are welcomed daily to learn about the cheetah. CCF's Center houses a state-of-the-art Cheetah Museum, veterinary clinic, genetics laboratory, and a Model Farm, providing the opportunity to practice and teach optimum methods of livestock and non-lethal farm management practices, acting as a showcase model of success.

Understanding how cheetahs live and where they live is very complex and includes human impact and ecology of the species, as well as the study of the overall health, genetic health, and disease risks. Long-term research on Namibian cheetahs has provided fundamental insights into the species' population biology and farmland ecology. This research continues to monitor the species and the affect of conservation initiatives.

CCF's Center is a global hub for research into the many aspects that contribute to a better understanding of the cheetah in the wild: health, genetics, reproduction, ecology, and behavior, among others. CCF's research is the basis for conservation education programs that have reached hundreds of thousands of students and youth in Namibia and elsewhere. In addition, CCF provides sanctuary to orphaned or injured cheetahs, many of which cannot be released back into the wild and act as educational ambassadors to thousands of visitors, students, and farmers every year.

Biomedical Research

CCF's biomedical research team has developed systematic studies. Each contact with a wild cheetah results in a full biomedical collection of blood, skin, and morphometric measurements. The cheetah is then ear tagged and released or placed in captivity if release is not possible. All collected samples are meticulously stored and serve as a reference database for future studies conducted at CCF or around the world.[4] Nearly 1,000 free-ranging cheetahs have been sampled, leading to one of the largest databases for any threatened species. Over 600 cheetahs have been released back into the wild.[5] The data has shown that conservation problems are not biological but have more to do with humans.

CCF facilitates the reintroduction/rehabilitation of wild cheetahs that have been captured on a farm as a perceived threat to livestock or confiscated by Namibian authorities. If the cheetah cannot be released immediately, CCF moves the animal to a secure pen at the CCF sanctuary. Every effort is made to care for the animal's health at the CCF veterinary clinic and, in the case of an adult cheetah, to reintroduce it to the wild as soon as practical. Only those animals that are not deemed mature or healthy enough to be released remain under the care of CCF's animal experts.

In the 1980's a research collaboration began an extensive study on the cheetah. The core team consisted of (from left): Dr. Steve O'Brien, geneticist, National Cancer Institute; Dr. Linda Munson, veterinary pathologist studying disease, University of California Davis; Jack Grisham, head of the American Zoo Association's (AZA) Cheetah Species Survival Plan (SSP), which coordinates the US zoo cheetah population; myself, International Cheetah Studbook Keeper and Founder and Executive Director of the Cheetah Conservation Fund; and Dr. David Wildt, Reproductive Physiologist, National Zoo, Smithsonian Institution.

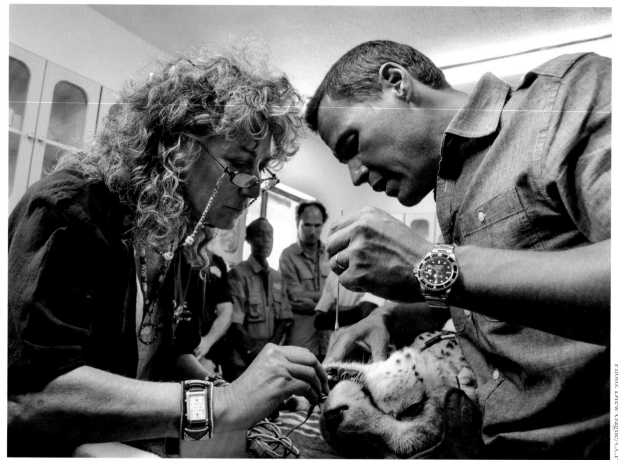

CCF has been a part of high priority research that monitors diseases in the wild population and measures stress responses in a variety of situations. Jeff Corwin, a CCF USA Trustee, helped me collect samples during one of his visits.

Infectious Disease

Cheetahs are known to be very susceptible to several feline diseases and are possibly more vulnerable due to the lack of heterogeneity in the population. As cheetahs transverse the farmlands where more villages occur the potential for disease transmission increases since cheetahs are increasingly likely to encounter domestic pets as they transverse the farmlands in their large home ranges.

Historically, it is assumed that these diseases did not affect wild cheetah populations. There is concern that infectious diseases may arise in wild animals that are in contact with domestic animals on farms, or trapped and held in captive facilities, and may transmit or acquire infectious diseases through these actions.[6]

Photo: Rick McKenna /CCF

Photo: CCF

◄ Census techniques vary depending on each country, region, habitat type, cheetah density, and land-owner attitudes. A combination of methods are used to provide an indication of cheetah numbers or trends. Though radio telemetry, data on home ranges, the area's most frequented by cheetahs on the farms, and times of the month or year they frequent specific areas gives farmers an insight as to why they may or may not have problems with cheetahs.

◄ To learn more about the behavior and movements of cheetah, farmers allow us to release radio-collared cheetahs back into the wild. Our success in working with farmers has resulted in fewer cheetahs being captured. On-going research is important to monitor population trends.

Census – How many cheetahs are there?

This is one of the most difficult questions to answer, as there are numerous difficulties associated with determining the overall population of wild cheetah and to understand their distribution which is necessary to identify and address threats to their long-term survival. This means developing censusing techniques so conservation management decisions can be made by government decision makers and focused on as highest priority needs.

Cheetahs are particularly difficult to census due to their large home ranges, which average over 800 sq. miles, and their regular movement across different farms from one day to another.[7] Cheetahs are very shy, mainly because of persecution on the farmlands where they have been shot, trapped, and chased. Wherever they occur they live in low densities.

CCF uses several indirect census techniques to determine population demography and density.[8] In Namibia, CCF's research team has been field-testing these techniques, which are then refined and extended to other habitat types.[9]

Why use dogs?

Dogs can smell much better than we can, as well as smell things humans aren't able to see. Dogs have 200 million scent receptors in their noses, unlike humans who only have 15 million. Therefore, dogs need only one particle of scent where humans would need 180,000 particles in order to identify a scent. The dogs' noses are so good, they only need a tiny piece of scat or particles to locate their objective.

Scat, or "black gold" provides researchers genetic identification through DNA, which can be extracted from the scat. DNA material is used to identify individuals using DNA derived microsatellites. CCF uses the cheetah scat as a part of a census technique to determine the presence of cheetahs in the area and to learn more about these individuals, their relatedness, and behavior.

Finn, one of CCF's detection dogs, finds cheetah scat on top of a termite mound and then sits to inform his trainer that he has found the scat. Scat detection dogs are trained similarly to narcotics or explosive-sniffing dogs but are trained to look for scat of target species. At CCF, it is cheetah. They usually work for a toy, like a ball, and will spend all day looking for scat if they know they will get to play with their toy when they find it. The use of a dog to find and detect individual cheetah scats in a field environment is invaluable.

Genetic Lab

Very few genetics laboratories exist in Africa, and transferring skills and knowledge to Africans is critical for African conservation.[10] CCF is committed to training. Dr. Ezequiel Fabiano, a CCF Senior Researcher, completed his Ph.D. in Conservation Genetics at CCF. Working with myself and Dr. Anne Schmidt-Küntzel, CCF's Assistant Director for Research and Senior Geneticist, we have trained many biologists from 12 cheetah-range countries in our genetics laboratory.

Does an animal in captivity represent the future? Linking zoos to the wild populations.
When one sees a cheetah in one of our world's zoological facilities, do we think that this cheetah represents the future of the species? How can these zoos help in our efforts to save the cheetah?

It is difficult to be concerned about the fate of an animal you have never seen. Although beautiful, seeing a film representation of a cheetah does not have anywhere near the same effect as seeing a live cheetah, watching it walk, smelling it, or even hearing it as it chirps or purrs. The usual response to such a real-life sight, whether in a zoo or in the wild, is emotional. Over the years the role of zoos has evolved with their most critical role in education, followed by research and conservation.[11]

The decline of African animals began in the 1960's. Today, many populations have declined by 80 percent or more during the last 100 years, and over 600 species of animals are teetering on the brink of extinction.[12]

Today's zoos are "Noah's Arks," working to maintain genetic diversity through captive breeding programs. These, coupled with the opportunities that captive populations provide for baseline research, has led to improvements in husbandry, thus increasing the longevity of animals in captivity.

Can captivity save the cheetah?

Zoos serve as educational centers, provide sanctuary to many endangered species, and have assisted in re-establishing some species in the wild.

The humans' love of cheetahs that has spanned thousands of years has caused their indiscriminate capture from the wild due to historically poor breeding in captivity. Until the 1960s, most zoos imported cheetahs from East Africa until the numbers of cheetahs declined. Namibia then became the major exporter of cheetahs. Today, more than 90 percent of all cheetahs in captivity are descendants of Namibian cheetahs.

In the early 1970s, the Convention of International Trade of Endangered Species (CITES) stopped the import of wild-caught animals into captivity. Then, zoos began working together to cooperatively breed and manage their rare species. Cooperative zoo management plans were developed in the United States and Europe, resulting in the North American SSP and the European Endangered Species Plan (EEP) for cheetahs.

The International Cheetah Studbook is one of the management tools. Studbooks register individual captive animals within a species and provide information about the genetic lineage or parentage of those animals, which provides the data for breeding recommendations to maintain the genetic diversity in captivity. I developed the International Cheetah Studbook in 1988 and work annually with cheetah facilities worldwide.[13]

CCF's Genome Resource ▶
Bank (GRB) contains
sperm samples on nearly
200 wild male cheetahs
we have worked on, which
will eventually enable the
transfer of genes to female
animals worldwide with-
out removing male animals
from their natural habitat.[14]

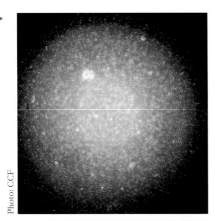

Photo: CCF

Applied Reproductive Techniques
Under the leadership of Dr. David Wildt,
Drs. JoGayle Howard, Adrienne Crosier, and
Pierre Comizzoli, all from the Smithsonian
Institution's National Zoological Park (NZP),
in collaboration with CCF, established optimal
procedures for freezing and thawing cheetah
sperm to create a functional Genome Resource
Bank (GRB) for future use in research and
conservation.

A GRB is a warehouse of biological materials
including sperm, blood products, skin, and other
tissues.

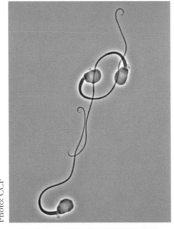

Photo: CCF

◀ Approximately 70-75
percent of sperm in a
male cheetah has super
large heads, tiny heads,
coiled or bent tails, which
are indicators of sterility
in all species.

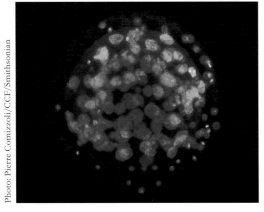

Photo: Pierre Comizzoli/CCF/Smithsonian

◀ The first blastocyst stage
embryos were developed
and frozen in CCF's
reproductive laboratory
in Namibia.

98

Raising Orphans

CCF cares for an average of 45 to 50 cheetahs at its Center. Each year, orphans are brought to CCF, where they can live up to 16 years of age or more. When cheetah cubs arrive they need varying amount of care depending on the their age and condition. Some will stay at CCF their entire lives and others have a chance to be returned to the wild.[15] All of them receive the best care, good diet, and regular exercise.

Most often, cubs come in between three to six months of age and are very wild. These cubs are monitored closely to make sure they settle and have no health problems. Some years, several orphans come in and CCF staff build groups of cheetahs by age. The orphans grow up together and become bonded as adopted families. As they get older, the males will be housed separately in age group coalitions and live together for the rest of their lives. Females also form social groups and stay bonded. Due to Namibian laws, CCF is not allowed to breed their captive cheetahs, but these cheetahs play an important role in on-going cheetah research.

Some cubs arrive at a younger age and are raised on bottles. Cow's milk is not an appropriate milk formula and can be fatal to the cubs. They require more attention and become habituated to their care takers. The nutrition for these growing cubs is critical. Often CCF receives cubs that have been given improper diets. It only takes a few days without proper care for calcium deficiencies to occur leading to hairline fractures or metabolic bone disease. Cheetah cubs need a high quality diet of lean meat and appropriate calcium and mineral supplements.

Cub care is extremely sensitive and around-the-clock care needs to be provided, as well as exercise. Cubs that have been hand raised become very tame and these cheetahs need even more attention and often become educational ambassadors.

Cheetahs have been used in zoo education for over 30 years. As a species that is non aggressive and easily habituated to human contact, cheetahs are often used as educational ambassadors.

Trained handlers present hand-raised cheetahs in a very professional way. These specially-raised cats, like CCF's Educational Ambassador Chewbaaka, usually spend most of their time purring when in public; their docile temperament proves very effective in their daily care and their mental stimulation.

At CCFs Research Center, 40 to 50 cheetahs are cared for in very large enclosures (10 to 100 acres). Cheetahs identified for rehabilitation have minimal exposure to people and are fed daily from the back of a truck where the meat is tossed to them. The cheetahs are exercised by running behind the truck keeping them healthy with a "wild" instinct.

What is a Sanctuary?

A wildlife sanctuary is a place that is set aside exclusively for wild animals. Sanctuaries are often established for the purpose of protecting rare or endangered species. Since it is not always possible to relocate animals or breed them in captivity, protecting their natural habitat is very important. Many countries recognize the value of their natural environment and local wildlife and, as a result, have made the establishment of sanctuaries a priority.

Human access to a wildlife sanctuary is usually restricted, and if people are allowed on the site they are escorted to ensure they do not disturb the animals or damage the environment. Biologists and other researchers work at sanctuaries to learn more about the animals that live there, but they tend to adopt a minimal interference approach to keep the animals as wild as possible.

Some sanctuaries also offer wildlife rehabilitation. In these instances, the refuge, like that of the Cheetah Conservation Fund in Namibia, agrees to take in injured and orphaned animals and nurse them back to health before releasing them into the sanctuary or back into the wild.

AFRICA: ROMANCING
THE REALITY

Africa: Romancing the Reality

The cheetah is walking two worlds in its race for survival: facing problems in protected areas and outside protected areas.

Borders are lines on maps that separate countries and people. These borders are a part of our world but wildlife doesn't recognize people's borders. Animals follow ancient migration patterns and seek suitable habitat that contains the right elements for their survival. This often puts them in conflict with people who inhabit the same land.

For the cheetah and other species, living within the borders of a protected park or game reserve like the Masai Mara in Kenya, the Serengeti National Park in Tanzania, or Kruger National Park in South Africa can mean the difference between life and death. The individual animals that live within protected lands are photographed by tourists and protected by rangers. This, however, can also cause a problem for some of these animals including the cheetah. The majority of cheetahs are not found in protected areas due to conflict with other larger predators. For cheetahs, there really are no borders of protection. In protected game reserves cheetahs often lose their kill or their cubs to larger and more aggressive predators like hyena and lions. Consequently, 90 percent of all cheetahs throughout their range are found living outside of protected lands.

Although Africa is a huge continent, there are approximately only 10 protected areas that are large enough to maintain genetically viable populations of cheetah. When cheetahs move out of protected lands, this leaves them vulnerable to humans, whose first priority is to protect their livelihoods.

Human-wildlife conflict and habitat loss are the biggest threats to cheetahs both inside and outside of the parks.

Although people from around the world travel to Africa to see cheetahs in the wild, the impact of tourism can affect cheetahs through the potential disturbance of hunts and separation of cubs and mothers.

What are the odds that a female cheetah could bring up all four cubs to adulthood?

Land fragmentation and human-wildlife conflict outside of parks are serious issues. As the human population continues to increase, there is a higher demand for land rights. This affects the cheetah as increased agricultural pressure and subdivision of land mean a decrease in available habitat for the cheetah and other wildlife species. Poaching, bush-meat trade, and the decreasing tolerance for wildlife in conflict with human development affect the prey base. In order to conserve the cheetah we must gain an understanding of the political issues and earn a trust within the communities that share their land with the wildlife.

The majority of cheetahs that are not found in protected areas face potential conflict with humans and livestock every day.

Throughout Africa, the majority of people who live alongside cheetahs are rural communal farmers whose livelihoods depend on their farm animals. Most of these farmers are poor and cannot afford to lose livestock to predators. Cheetahs, to these farmers, are not beautiful icons of speed and elegance; they are a nuisance and a threat. CCF's work has demonstrated the importance of addressing the livelihoods of the human communities living alongside cheetahs. By reducing their livestock losses and increasing their farm's productivity, farmers will save cheetahs instead of killing them.

Throughout much of Africa, changes in these arid ecosystems in favor of human needs have created problems for the rural farmers, mainly through overgrazing leading to desertification. This leaves limited grazing for wildlife. Ultimately, the survival of the cheetah depends on re-balancing the ecosystem and habitat to provide sufficient natural prey for cheetahs and other wildlife.[16]

However, there may be forces of nature that we cannot predict or manage and that affect cheetah survival, such as climate change. Climate change is expected to negatively affect agriculture and wildlife as the rangelands become drier and vegetation is altered throughout the cheetah's arid rangelands.[17] This will affect the distribution and abundance of prey species and the migratory nature of most game in arid areas will require that large tracks of land are kept intact. To this end, the development of conservancy type complexes will be critical.

The realities of what is needed for the cheetah to survive lies in the understanding of what is needed for human survival. High populations, poverty, lack of education and resources, unemployment, and malnutrition continue as the current population of the African continent continues to grow. As the human population grows, wildlife and the natural world pay the price as wildlife habitat is developed, air and water are polluted, and the climate crisis deepens.

◀ Humans and livestock need grazing space and water; however, these resources are becoming very limited throughout the cheetah's range. Most areas where cheetahs are found are very arid.

If girls in the developing world get seven or more years of school, they will marry four years later and have 2.2 fewer children. Every year a girl completes in school decreases infant mortality by 5-10 percent.

Education throughout Africa, particularly the empowerment of women and girls, is critical to achieve healthier ecosystems. As a woman running a research center in Africa, I take women's issues very seriously. Girls represent 54 percent of all the 32 million children out of school in Sub-Saharan Africa. For the rural poor, household chores outweigh the benefits of sending the girls to school. More than 50 percent less girls will be educated than boys.

It has been seen that with each year of schooling, women's wages are boosted by 10 to 20 percent, women become more involved in government and community activities, and women become more concerned about the degradation of the environment.

Although people are the problem in today's world, people are the solution as well. In Africa the cheetah and other wildlife species in its ecosystem live with a variety of African tribes, each having a different culture and each approaching development, wildlife, agriculture, and tourism in different ways.

The Maasai for centuries have developed *boma*, or corral-systems, which are scattered throughout the Maasai land.

In Kenya, the Samburu people in the north are cousins of the Maasai, which live in southern Kenya and Tanzania. Both tribes are semi-nomadic and herd their livestock. Their livestock is their wealth, the same as that of the Herero and Himba in Namibia and Botswana. Therefore, their priority for grazing lands is their cattle, goats, and sheep. In some cultures wildlife has no value as it competes for grazing.

Community-based natural resource management non-governmental organizations (NGOs) have been working with many of these communities in Africa to develop integrated programs incorporating tourism development and economic incentives, which can diversify their livelihoods.

The small stock remains at the main homesteads, or *bomas*, with families, while the young *morani* warriors herd their cattle into seasonal grazing areas. The elders control the movement of their livestock as they understand the dynamics of the grasslands, as well as the wildlife and livestock that share it. This land is critical to the seasonal migrations of wildlife. The traditional Maasai system of livestock and land management has tolerance for wildlife. Their flocks and herds are locked in the corral each evening, leaving the unfenced land for the wildlife. During the day, wildlife grazes next to the Maasai cattle, goats, and sheep.

Demand for firewood has led to depletions of forests resulting in deforestation and desertification.

Predators are very wary of the Maasai and usually keep their distance. The Maasai are not traditionally agriculturists but the times are changing. This change will affect cheetahs and many other wildlife species in this vast African landscape.

Over the past 35 years these semi-arid grazing lands are being converted by Maasai to cropland to diversify their income. However, at the same time, they are expanding their livestock herds. The cultivation of the land has caused extensive soil erosion and many of the best dry season pastures and watering areas have been converted into strictly wildlife areas where they are no longer allowed. The pressure on the land is enormous.

Many of the crop-growing Maasai consider most wildlife species just another agricultural pest. As the Maasai become wealthier they acquire larger herds of livestock, but as the herds increase the grazing becomes less abundant and the Maasai tradition of tolerance for wildlife diminishes.

As the grasslands shrink, so do the options for wildlife and the cheetah. Although their grasslands were better managed traditionally with the integration of wildlife management strategies, today there is little attention to sustainable farming or appropriate soil and water conservation. These environmental issues, combined with the Maasai cattle culture, will increasingly continue to pose challenges for long-term cheetah survival in this important region of Africa and, unlike in Namibia, wildlife management is still not considered as sound an investment as is agriculture.

Firewood is the equivalent to the poor people's electricity. It provides fire for cooking and heat to keep warm. One of the products from wood is unsustainable charcoal production. The demand for charcoal is higher as populations and costs of alternative energy sources increase. In Tanzania alone, over 800 acres of forest land is destroyed daily. Increased charcoal consumption in Africa's major cities and the use of traditional kilns have resulted in the destruction and depletion of forests throughout Sub-Saharan Africa, further depredating habitats and the livelihoods of rural people.

Bush Encroachment

 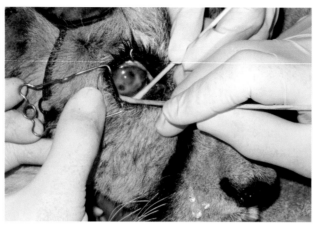 

Photo: Laurie Marker/CCF

Photo: Laurie Marker/CCF

Bush encroachment is a form of desertification caused by overgrazing arid landscapes causing thickened thornbush. It has led to a unique ecological threat to the cheetah in Namibia on traditionally open savanna lands where cheetahs hunt using their natural advantage: speed.

Bush encroachment changes the habitat and, thus, the mix of wildlife and cheetah-prey species.

The increase in bush encroachment is caused by a century of livestock overgrazing, exacerbated by drought cycles in the arid farmland regions. Bush encroachment, which covers over 60 million acres of cattle and livestock farmland in Namibia or nearly one third of the country, has been responsible for reducing the carrying capacity of the farmland for livestock and wild game,

and has reduced farmers' income and Namibia's economy, with losses estimated at over US$150 million per year.

For cheetahs, bush encroachment has caused two main problems. First, farmers with encroached land tend to kill more cheetahs and other predators. Secondly, the cheetah's habitat has gone from an open savanna bush veld to a thickened thorn bush savanna that is nearly impenetrable. As the cheetah sprints through this modified habitat its eyes often become scratched by the thorns resulting in long-term damage to its sight, which is critical to its hunting ability. With impaired eyesight, cheetahs are likely to become problem animals and seek livestock over wildlife, causing conflict with humans.

Today, one can visually see the borders between farmlands and national parks.

Cheetahs don't see property lines but farmers and communities do. Settlements and cultivation create large areas of land where wildlife cannot pass through at all. Droughts and over-usage of land have resulted in food and water shortages. Studies in Kenya show that human densities in the country have led to increased subdivision of land which was once open for animal movements and today is full of fences. For decades, livestock farmers throughout Africa have trapped and killed cheetahs preemptively to protect their livestock. Although on farmlands cheetahs do not have to compete with other large predators as they do in protected areas, farmers have systematically removed thousands of cheetahs from across their range. In Namibia alone, the cheetah population was halved in the 1980's where farmers removed nearly 7,000 cheetahs.

Tourism – Everyone who comes to Africa on a safari wants to see a cheetah.

Romance equals the beauty and vast open plains of Africa's pristine protected area networks, like the Masai Mara, and is what most people think of when they think of cheetahs in Africa.

However, the reality is harsh; the area is no longer what it once was. Tourism helps to bring international attention to cheetahs, but crowds of multiple vehicles surrounding cheetahs and other wildlife can have a negative impact on their survival. In the wild, every action and every move by all species is a matter of life and death. Wildlife must breed, feed, and maintain a territory. The disruption of a mating event, a hunt, or getting too close to a mother with offspring can have lasting and damaging effects on the delicate balance of life in the wild.

The harassment of wildlife species by tourism doesn't get much attention. Researchers see it day after day, year after year. The tourism industry is under pressure to provide close-up encounters with predators because this is the image visitors have seen in wildlife documentaries. The challenge is to educate tourists so that they understand that the close encounter with wildlife they crave actually does harm to the animals.

Tourists rely on the tour operator to do the right thing. However, the tourists need to be made aware of the real harm they can do and have a responsibility to stop their safari guides from conducting themselves improperly. Drivers should not get close enough to allow cheetahs to climb on their vehicle or allow cubs to play on or around their vehicles.

Cheetahs hunt in the early morning and late afternoon when most tourists are out on game drives. The safari guides in their minibuses will sometimes move between the cheetah and its prey so the tourists can get a better view. This interferes with the cheetahs' hunts and can separate mother from cubs.

Cheetahs are not aggressive and their nature makes them easily habituated. To get a better view of the habitat, cheetahs often jump on vehicle hoods to see prey over long grass or the cubs play on hoods and hide from each other under the vehicles or on the tires. This means the drivers need to be extra careful as they can run over a cub or separate cubs from their mothers.

Photo: Elliott Neep

Several of Kenya's protected areas suffer from such intrusions as off-road driving, excessive noise, and frequent harassment of wildlife. Research conducted in the Masai Mara recorded that nearly 30 percent of cheetah sightings had over 20 vehicles surrounding it and over 50 percent of these vehicles were less than 30 yards from the cheetahs with nearly 60 percent being noisy (hooting, reversing, and revving engines) with the tourists and drivers shouting or talking very loudly. The busiest time for tourist vehicles is between 4:00 and 6:30pm, which was the highest time of hunting for cheetahs.

Predators are extremely aware of tourists and their vehicles and use them to their advantage. If a cheetah has made a kill it will most certainly lose it if vehicles are present, since other predators, in particular hyenas, lions, and jackals, are alerted by the tourists. If the cheetah has cubs this could be one of the most dangerous situations, as their cubs could get killed or separated from them.

Most wildlife documentaries might lead people to think that it is okay to drive right up to a hunting cheetah. However, it is important to note that professional film crews have developed very unobtrusive methods to capture these fascinating scenes. The global tourism operators need to be the collaborative effort between the government departments and tour operators with the responsibility on the tourist facilities to help support appropriate behavior.[18]

Many cheetahs are reported with sarcoptic mange and are treated. The high incidence of sarcoptic mange in cheetahs in the Masai Mara which has been linked to stress caused by tourism vehicles. Documenting the level of stress among the Masai Mara cheetahs has helped us to understand how human-induced stress can affect their health and population stability. Chronic stress induces immuno-suppression, which in cheetahs has been found to contribute to a high occurrence of uncommon diseases, like manage. Quantifying cheetahs' stress levels helps develop conservation decisions and policies. Although environmental ethics dictate noninterference in natural-caused events, authorities in the Mara ecosystem routinely treat many cheetah diseases and injuries caused by humans.

Cheetahs are the best hunters but have no way to defend their kills
from larger predators like hyenas and lions and must just walk away.

Cheetahs are considered the best hunter of the savanna, but this does not guarantee the cheetah a meal.

Catching and killing their prey and keeping it are two different matters. Due to their smaller size and light weight body, cheetahs are submissive and shy and easily chased from their kill by other predators. They successfully kill one in 10 hunts, using a huge, energy-depleting burst of speed, but 50 percent of their kills are then snatched right out of their grasp by competing predators such as lions, leopards, or spotted hyenas.

Cheetahs must eat fast as groups of vultures and jackals will come take their share of the kill. Afterwards, the smaller animals including mongoose, porcupines, civet, genet cats, and birds will have a meal before the insects come. And so, the cheetah helps to feed other animals which are important in the ecological cycle.

◀ Egyptian vulture at kill.

◀ Egyptian mongoose eating meat.

◀ Even jackals and vultures can chase the cheetah from its kill.

Where did all the prey go?

As a selective hunter, the cheetah plays a major role in the health of prey populations by seeking the oldest and weakest animal from a herd. This allows the strongest to survive and continue the evolutionary process since these stronger animals can then pass on their genes to strengthen the species as a whole.

Many farmers fail to acknowledge the role predators play in the ecosystem. Africa's predator and prey species evolved together and without one the other could not have developed. The hunting of game by predators results in abundant and diverse eco-systems that we can still see today. The role of predators is critical. Without them, game species would be significantly less healthy since the weaker animals that are usually selected by predators would instead survive to reproduce. Wildlife is one of Africa's most valuable resources and gives it its unique image. Predators are vital to the health of our wildlife and are an integral part of what attracts tourists to Africa.

Impalas in rainstorm.

◀ Thomson's gazelles at sunset.

There is considerable variation in cheetah prey, ranging from Thomson's gazelle on the Serengeti plains, impala in Kruger National Park, to kudu, gerenuk, and dik-dik in the arid areas of northern Kenya. Other species reported as prey include puku, kob and oribi, springbok, wildebeest, hare, and seasonally a large proportion of prey consumed consists of immature calves. In the north central livestock farmlands of Namibia, kudu, warthog, red hartebeest, gemsbok, steenbok, and duiker have been reported as regular prey species. Cheetahs have a preferred prey range of 20 to 123lbs with an average of 60lbs.

But, where has all their prey gone?
In Namibia, due to a variety of circumstances in the 1980's, including the reduction of wildlife populations due to a severe drought and the continued over-stocking of livestock on rangelands, cheetah populations came into even greater conflict with farmers. During this same period, 80 percent of kudu, a key prey species for the cheetah, died off due to an outbreak of rabies. As a result of these events the cheetah resorted to greater predation of livestock instigating an all-out war towards the cheetah by farmers. By the latter part of the 1980's, the cheetah population had been reduced by more than half. Today, kudu rabies continues to be a problem; however, other wildlife in Namibia has made a comeback and over 80 percent is found outside of protected areas on livestock farmlands.

Throughout southern Africa droughts play a role in the reduction of game as farmers catch or kill more of the game during these times to save pastures for livestock and are also less tolerant of any conflict with predators if these resort to preying upon livestock. Therefore, predators like African wild dogs and cheetahs need to cover even larger areas in order to find appropriate prey. This then places them in potentially more conflict with farmers. However, research has shown that where there is enough prey, predators like the cheetahs favor natural prey over livestock.

South African Wildlife – A Different Game

In southern Africa, the increase of game-fenced farms, protected by 10-foot tall fences with 21 wires, stop the natural movement of wild game. Although increasing their potential for appropriate prey for cheetahs, game farmers have little tolerance for cheetahs on their farms. This scenario places greater pressure on the cheetah's habitat needs and reduces the numbers of prey available for them, thus increasing the likelihood of livestock depredation by cheetahs and, in consequence, the level of farmer-cheetah conflict.

Today, thousands of miles of game-fenced farms have been erected in southern Africa. Many game farmers also stock exotic game species on their land for trophy hunters; these animals are not only more valuable than indigenous game but also more liable to predation than the better-adapted indigenous game species. Even a relatively low level of predation upon expensive, non-native exotic game can have

economic impacts upon farmers that they are unwilling to tolerate.[19]

The greatest annual migration of wildlife occurs in Kenya and Tanzania. Each year 1.5 million wildebeest and 300,000 zebra, along with other antelope and predators, move between the Serengeti Plains in Tanzania to the Masai Mara in Kenya. Each year a large number of animals don't survive the migration and fall prey to large predators, thus continuing the cycle of life.

Africa is endowed with highly diverse species of fauna and flora. Savannas, which are the richest grasslands in the world, are the most extensive ecosystems in Africa. They support many indigenous plants and animals, as well as the world's largest concentration of large mammals such as elephants, wildebeests, buffalo, rhinoceros, giraffes, lion, leopards, cheetah, zebras, hippopotami, kudus, springbok, and oryx.

Illegal trade is one of the greatest pressures on wildlife species.

In Africa today, elephants, rhinos, and other animals long identified with this continent are dying. Poaching is one reason; loss of habitat caused by a growing human population encroaching on areas once inhabited by the free-ranging animals is another. But when the animals in Kenya, for example, suffer, so does the country, which depends heavily on income from international tourists. Kenya's wildlife has been reduced by 50 percent in the past 25 years.

Not that long ago, when the elephant herds expanded they were able to migrate to new areas. Now, it's very rare for elephants to still range beyond a park's borders. In most areas of the Masai Mara and other noted game reserves, the elephants run headlong into problems when they reach the park's boundary and run into developed areas. They become potential victims to farmers, hunters, and poachers.

Poaching is a very serious problem for rhinoceros, both black and white, which are the fastest diminishing large mammal on the planet. These prehistoric looking large animals are being killed for their horns at what has been described as an "unstoppable rate." In Asia, ground rhino horn is believed to be a cure for cancer and used for other illnesses, and the illegally traded horn is fetching more than $30,000 a pound on the world market.

At the turn of the century, a million rhinos inhabited all of the Sub-Saharan Africa; in the past few years, rhino populations have been exterminated in nine of those countries. In the 1960s, an estimated 20,000 black rhino lived in Kenya alone. Today this country has only a fragmented rhino population numbering only a few hundred.[20]

World estimates put the global black rhino population at about 5,000. This species' population has decreased 90 percent since the 1960s and if we don't actively work to save every one of them their time will run out.

Predators also are the victim of poaching. Whether directly hunted for their pelts or accidentally killed by walking into a snare which has been set for local antelope for bush meat. Snares indiscriminately kill anything that walks into them.

Anti-poaching teams are on patrol daily in the Masai Mara.

Throughout Africa, anti-poaching teams are notoriously underfunded and outnumbered by the poachers. Much of the poaching is done with snares. On a routine patrol a team may find over 200 snares in a single day. In some of the parks in west Africa where poaching has become organized crime, wildlife rangers suit up with assault rifles, machine guns, and rocket-propelled grenades each day as they go into their parks to protect the wildlife. It's becoming a battleground vs. a wildlife park.

Much of the poaching that goes on is not for ivory or rhino horn but for meat.
In many areas of Africa there is a huge commercial bush meat trade. This
poacher is standing in front of his camp. He and his team of 12 were caught
poaching wildebeest, Thompson's gazelle, and impala.

The raw ivory trade moves through African elephant-range states to transit countries, then on to processing centers, most often in Asia, with China being the world's largest consumer of illegal ivory and the United States the second largest market for wildlife products. Carved ivory is found in markets in Africa, Asia, and other parts of the planet, including ivory items for the tourist curio trade which is illegal.

Reports show that up to 100 elephants are killed every day in Africa.

In 2012, 30,000 elephants in Africa were killed for their tusks. Unlike meat poachers, elephant and rhino poaching is very sophisticated. Is killing animals for accessories, souvenirs, and other trinkets worth eliminating some of the rarest species on earth? As elephants, rhinos, giraffes, tigers, and other wildlife face declining numbers action is needed today. CCF is a founding member of the Coalition Against Wildlife Trafficking (CAWT) which is working on political change to stop this illegal trade. Often criminal syndicates deploy advanced technologies ranging from night vision scopes, silenced weapons, darting equipment, and helicopters to carry out their mission. Although the practice of poaching wildlife for economic gain is nothing new it has now evolved into a revenue source for crime syndicates and terrorist organizations, with consequences not just for wildlife but for public safety and national security. The International Conservation Caucus Foundation (ICCF), of which CCF is a founding member, works to educate the US Congress to understand the issues affecting wildlife and threats linked to illegal trade.

But where has all their prey gone?

The poaching of rhinos and elephants for their horns and tusks represents an urgent crisis that must be addressed, and, based on credible reports, live cheetahs for the illegal pet trade and other endangered species are being smuggled along with elephant tusks.

Somalia, Africa's most lawless country for more than 20 years without a functioning government, is supporting militants, gunrunners, and pirates with the ivory and illegal wildlife trade, like the live sale of cheetah cubs. They are infiltrating northern Kenya and have encouraged villagers along the border to help. The port of Kismayo, a known smuggling hub, is believed to be from where many cheetahs are illegally transported.

In northern Africa, the rarity of the prey is directly linked to the rarity of the Saharan or desert cheetah, as both the predator and the prey are listed as critically endangered species by the IUCN Red List. The Saharan cheetah can still be found in small numbers in Algeria (Ahaggar and Tassili N'Ajjer), Niger (Termit and Aïr), and possibly also in Mali, Chad, and Mauritania, with their main threats being the increased lack of suitable prey due to poaching, over hunting, and conflict with herders over stock harassment and killing. These cheetahs are living primarily on hare but are known to attack and kill young camels and goats, provoking retaliation from their owners.

Illegal Trade of Cheetahs

CCF has been involved in fighting the illegal pet trade in cheetahs since 2005 when it organized the rescue of cheetah cubs found tied up at a storefront in a small village in Ethiopia. Since then, we have monitored cases of illegal cheetah trafficking assisting with confiscations through the proper authorities whenever possible.

Throughout the Arabian Peninsula many cheetahs and other exotic animals are purchased illegally and kept as pets. This practice undermines the survival of the species. Cheetahs are one of the most popular exotic pets in that region, and there is a huge demand and the "in thing" among some residents. CCF has been at the forefront of these issues.[21]

Addressing the complex and urgent issue of illegal cheetah trafficking requires multiple, concerted appraoches. As such, CCF encourages government institutions and NGO's concerned with illegal wildlife trafficking to join forces and do the following: include measures to stop the illegal live pet trade when dealing with the international community around the illegal wildlife trade and discourage the keeping of cheetahs as pets or as roadside attractions.

The buying public must understand that very often the cheetah cubs they purchase, even with claims of having proper paperwork are in fact, poached from the wild. The wild cheetah population cannot sustain these losses.

CCF estimates that at most one in six smuggled cubs survive the process of being transported to a buyer due to malnutrition or inadequate treatment. In all likelihood, mother cheetahs are killed to obtain cubs for the illegal pet trade. The wild cheetah population cannot sustain these losses.

The majority of cases are reported in the Horn of Africa countries of Djibouti, Somalia, Ethiopia, and Somaliland.[22] Of these countries, only Ethiopia and Somalia still have small, wild cheetah populations. Illegal capture is occurring mostly in Ethiopia, Somalia, and northern Kenya, from where the animals are then transported to be sold in the Arabian Peninsula on a regular basis. Once "bought," the chances of survival to over five months of age is very low and, if they do survive, most do not live over two years of age.

CCF urges concerned individuals, governments, and institutions around the world to unify efforts aimed at finding solutions for dealing with illegally-obtained cheetahs and to undertake education efforts aimed at reducing demand for cheetahs as pets.[23]

Photo: Laurie Marker/CCF

CHANGING THE FACE
OF AFRICA

Saving the cheetah means changing the world.

As human populations continue to rise, agriculture claims more and more land leading to livestock-wildlife conflicts. A new form of farming is needed; the Future Farmers of Africa where conservancies practice integrated systems that can support food for people and habitat for wildlife. Cheetahs can have a place in the future.

Through educational outreach programs farmers learn livestock management techniques so that they don't have "problem" animals catching livestock, thus reducing the need to trap or shoot cheetahs on their farms and reversing the historical belief that the only good cheetah is a dead cheetah. Farmers are taught about livestock health and management along with grasslands, wildlife, and basic principles of ecology. Ancient breeds of livestock guarding dogs from Turkey the Anatolian shepherd and Kangal have shown huge success. Dogs donated to livestock farmers by the Cheetah Conservation Fund deter cheetahs and other predators from preying on livestock.

Through Future Farmers of Africa habitats can be restored, farmers can have better livelihoods, and cheetahs can share the land. Through proper land use planning there will be areas where cheetah reintroductions can take place. Countries like India, where the cheetah was revered by maharajahs and loved to extinction in the past century, today plan reintroducing cheetahs to restore eco-systems. The Cheetah Conservation Fund has developed strategies to rehabilitate cheetahs into the wild; however, each reintroduction is difficult and requires careful planning and suitable habitat.

In many areas throughout the cheetah's range poaching is decimating our wildlife populations for food and profit. The illegal wildlife trade is in the same league as arms and drug smuggling. Live trade in cheetah cubs is a growing business in the Arabian Peninsula, with only one in six cheetahs surviving the ordeal.

A future for the cheetah will include large landscapes with grasslands that will support livestock and wildlife. Stable governments will support policies that include healthy ecosystems for the cheetah and people. Saving the cheetah means changing the world.

◀ This ancient breed of guarding dog comes from Turkey. At CCF's Model Farm, the livestock guarding dogs work beside and independently from the small stock herders. Their loud bark alerts any predators in the area and predators, like cheetahs, avoid the area where there is livestock and a livestock guarding dog.

Livestock Guarding Dogs – Growing Up

As a non-lethal solution for predator control, CCF began a livestock guarding dog program in 1994 with Anatolian shepherd and Kangal dogs. These are Turkish breeds used for over 6,000 years to protect sheep from wolves. Their short-hair coat allows these breeds to adapt to the fluctuating temperatures on the Anatolian Plateau. Like in Namibia, temperatures there can vary by 40 degrees in the course of a day. This breed is also an independent thinking dog and is used to work unattended over vast areas.

The puppies are born in the corral where they grow up with the livestock they will be protecting when they get older. In the 20 years since the program began, CCF has bred and placed nearly 500 dogs with both commercial and communal Namibian farmers. Farmers have reported large declines in livestock losses since receiving a dog. The puppies become attentive to their stock and are the "smart" member of the herd making them trustworthy with their flocks. This is a bonding period, from which they will grow up to become gentle protectors of their charges. A high level of attentiveness to the livestock and the amount of care given by the farmer are key components to the effectiveness of a guarding dog.

These Anatolian shepherd livestock guarding dog puppies are only three weeks old. When they reach ten weeks of age they will be given to local Namibian farmers where they will grow up with their flocks to protect the livestock from predators.

Because the dogs are very effective at protecting and monitoring a herd, farmers can run their farms more efficiently with less personnel. One positive side effect where CCF dogs are in use is that farmers can reduce the amount of time their children watch the herds, allowing them to go to school more frequently.

Going to Farms

Photo: Harry Harrington/CCF

When the puppies are about 10 weeks of age they are transported to their new homes to continue bonding with the flocks they will protect for the rest of their lives.

CCF educators visit the puppies regularly until they are 18 months old to make sure that the early training and care continues appropriately and then annually thereafter to monitor their effectiveness.[24]

Livestock guarding dogs are just one of the simple 'predator-friendly' farming methods advocated by CCF. The use of livestock guarding dogs in Namibia has proven to be a useful and economically beneficial method of livestock protection. CCF's Livestock Guarding Dog Program has been a success; our research has shown that seven out of 10 farmers who keep a guarding dog with their flocks report from 80 to 100 percent fewer losses.

Protect and Kids Can Go to School

Photo: Harry Harrington/CCF

The addition of a livestock guarding dog allows the protection of the herds as well as the children.

Rural African children are often entrusted with herding their families' goats and sheep. These children are often confronted with predators or other dangers in the bush. If dangers occur, the children often run to the safety of their home leaving the herd unattended. The dogs do not grow up as a pet and are always with the herd. As they grow, they learn the power of their loud bark. They learn to place themselves between the predator and livestock and as they continue to mature they become as large as the predators they are protecting against, and are able to force the predators to move away or avoid the area where the dogs and livestock are grazing. If necessary the dog will attack to protect its livestock "family".

Photo: Christophe LePetit/CCF

CCF believes that changing the perception that cheetahs pose a significant threat to livelihoods is of vital importance, as research has shown that the levels of tolerance toward predators can be increased through awareness-building, education, and economic development.

Helping farmers see cheetahs through our eyes includes training programs used to educate farmers in livestock health and basic ecology.

In the 1980s, local Namibian farmers decimated the cheetah population, trapping and shooting thousands of animals based on the belief that such acts were necessary to protect their livestock and their livelihoods. CCF, from its inception in 1990, has been addressing this issue head on, by developing ways to train farmers in livestock management techniques that not only address wildlife concerns but make farms more profitable. CCF's Future Farmers of Africa (FFA) program teaches integrated conservation, livestock, and wildlife management techniques to present and future land users and managers.

Over 80 percent of Namibia's wildlife lives on farmland and therefore, integrated livestock-wildlife management training for farmers has the greatest impact on conserving Namibia's wildlife.

CCF has developed agricultural, ecological, and economic training initiatives and educational modules that are specifically designed to achieve the aforementioned goals for the benefit of farmers, the habitat, and the future of Namibia. These programs, called Future Farmers of Africa, are models for other cheetah range countries.[25]

A farmer with a healthy herd and healthy land-use practices has measures in place to protect livestock and is less likely to trap or kill cheetahs, either in retaliation or to prevent predation.

CCF's training courses for farmers and farm workers cover topics that include correct predator spore identification as shown by CCF's chief ecologist, Matti Nghikembua, livestock management to reduce losses, livestock health and husbandry, farm management, and methods for non-lethal predator control, such as the use of Anatolian shepherd or Kangal livestock guarding dogs.

By reaching out to school learners through CCF's FFA, all stakeholders are trained in best practices in predator-friendly livestock and grasslands management.

Management of Livestock

Conservation research, education, and wise management of livestock and wildlife populations are all critical to the survival of cheetah and other predators in Africa and throughout the world. Since Namibia's wildlife is in the hands of landowners, strategies to sustain populations of wildlife for the future have been developed in conjunction with livestock management through the promotion of conservancies. Conservancies, on both communal and commercial lands, are collaborative partnerships of neighboring farmers who work together to develop and implement sustainable livestock and wildlife management systems. There are over 75 communal and 20 commercial conservancies in Namibia, which work as integrative systems combining food for people and habitat for wildlife, allowing cheetahs to have a place in the future.

Photo: Laurie Marker/CCF

Photo: Laurie Marker/CCF

Farmland Stewardship –
Conservancies increase opportunities for communities.

Conservation biologists increasingly underscore that protected areas alone are simply not large enough to sustain the wildlife they were created to protect. This is particularly true for the cheetah that does not thrive in protected areas due to the increased competition with other large predators. Therefore, a focus on the conservation of private land is crucial.

Farmland ecosystems throughout the cheetah's range will need on-going conservation strategies that include habitat viability for the cheetah and its prey. These can be integrated with managed livestock. The Namibian Conservancy model is being exported to other countries to help in the diversification of livelihoods.[26]

Conservancies are one of the most important solutions for cheetah's survival in Namibia as they promote sustainable management of natural resources and development of responsible eco-tourism. Conservancies give communities a vested interest in the welfare of local wildlife by giving them control over the economic benefits from wildlife populations. As a result, the country has fewer problems with poaching and is committed to growing its eco-tourism industry to maximize benefits to communities, many of which are extremely rural and have few other opportunities for economic development. The establishment of conservancies has helped to decrease human-wildlife conflict and save the cheetah.

Photo: ICS/DoE/CACP/UNDP/Panthera

Camera traps have been set up in various reserves in Iran
to learn more about this critically endangered species.
Photos of cheetahs have helped identify individuals.
The identification of various cheetahs have led to
conservation initiatives with the support of the IUCN
Cat Specialist Group, Panthera, Wildlife Conservation
Society (WCS), UNDP, the Iranian government,
and CCF.

Dr. Laurie Marker in Iran.

Dr. Laurie Marker and team in Algeria.

Managing Populations Globally

In Iran I worked with conservation teams to better understand the threats to the cheetah and helped recommend short and long-term plans for conservation strategies.

The Iranian Cheetah Society (ICS) was developed as a non-government organization. Working with the Conservation of the Asiatic Cheetah Project (CACP), a joint partnership between the Iranian Department of Environment (DOE) and United Nations Development Programme (UNDP). ICS monitors and develops strategies to grow this critically endangered population. I have visited Iran a few times and have worked with our partners there to create strategies including buying out livestock herders who have established themselves in protected areas and community education programs. These reserves are the last refuges for the critically endangered Asiatic cheetah population.

I have traveled to Algeria several times to help develop conservation strategies for the cheetah in the country and to meet with the local Tuareg, who, historically, are a nomadic tribe in the region. There is a small population of cheetah remaining in the l'Ahaggar and Tassili National Parks in southern Algeria.

The Sahara is a complex mosaic of landscapes not just miles and miles of endless sand, as it is often thought. The region includes some of the biggest grasslands and highest mountain ranges in Africa. These fragile landscapes and critical wildlife habitats need strategies for their sustainable use, including communication and partnerships with the people that use the land and its resources, as well as tools to assist in conservation measures.

The Concepts of Rehabilitation

Photo: Rob Thompson/CCF

Prior to the soft release, the cheetahs are given extensive medical examinations and fitted with a satellite collar that allows for close monitoring.

Going full circle, CCF's research continues in cheetah rehabilitation and reintroduction back into the wild. We are often called to relocate cheetahs that have been trapped by farmers or to pick up cheetahs that the government deems are being held illegally or in unhealthy conditions. These animals are brought to CCF, provided with medical attention, and released immediately within an appropriate release site when deemed healthy and old enough to survive on their own. Cheetahs that cannot be released are provided sanctuary in large enclosures at CCF. Many of these cheetahs might be releasable into the wild once they are old enough if they have maintained a wild disposition. Reintroduction of cheetahs orphaned at an early age is difficult even if their natural habitats are restored due to the absence of survival techniques which are usually passed from mothers to offspring. For cheetahs, the first months with their mother are crucial to learn the skills they need to survive in the wild. CCF has developed a sound process for allowing wild-born cheetahs to rehabilitate (or relearn) survival skills after being in captivity for a sustained period.

Photo: Pete Oxford/ Minden Pictures

Over 70 percent of CCF's rehabilitated cheetahs have succeeded in learning to live in the wild.

Carefully identified candidates, after living in large natural compounds of up to 200 acres, are soft released in CCF's 8,000-acre Bellebenno game camp, which is abundant with prey species.

Being semi-habituated, they are fed until they are hunting for themselves regularly. CCF's research shows that most of these selected cheetahs learn to hunt and adapt to a free-ranging lifestyle: a process that can take anywhere from a number of weeks to a number of months. CCF's research on reintroduction is important to the future of

the cheetah as it shows that the process is viable and can be modified as needed. The expected outcome is a proven process for reintroduction that can be emulated in other range countries. Through this research, CCF can more rapidly help cheetahs reconnect fragmented populations so that the gene pool can be diversified as much as possible. If successful, potentially important cheetah populations in other range countries could be re-established within the next few years.[27]

Outside Namibia, CCF has been consulting with former cheetah-range countries, India and Uzbekistan, where the cheetah has been extinct for decades, about reintroducing cheetahs into those countries. CCF acts as an advisor. Possibly, some of CCF's sanctuary cheetahs could be reintroduced in these countries pending approval by the relevant governments and authorities. Reintroductions can only be successful in areas that can support adequate prey populations. Critical components of the overall program include land-use planning and livestock management, as well as the population dynamics of the prey base and government will. The cheetah is a survivor and it could survive again in India and other countries where the cheetah has become recently extinct.

◀ Will this mother be able to raise her cubs to adulthood in the face of all these threats? With luck and hard work, along with applied conservation and government support, there will be habitat for this mother to raise her cubs to adulthood without all these threats.

CHEETAHSCAPES

Cheetahscapes

In Namibia, farmers' attitudes and behaviors towards cheetah have changed since CCF began its ongoing research in 1990. Many farmers no longer think of the cheetah on their lands as a direct threat to their livelihoods, and the number of cheetahs being removed from their farms has declined. Although some farmers still perceive the cheetah to be a threat to income and livestock, their tolerance has increased.

The future of the cheetah will require enhancing the livelihoods of the human communities that live alongside them. These include developing alternative income sources, such as eco-tourism, economic incentives for predator-friendly products, or alternative value-added agricultural products like goat's cheese. At the same time, grasslands can be managed in such a way that the habitat can support not only livestock but also wildlife to promote tourism.

At CCF's Model Farm, local farmers and students are being trained in developing products such as goat cheese, ice cream, and fudge, to demonstrate how a collaborative, community-based model of conservation can benefit the community as a whole.

The important difference between these efforts and the efforts of conservation in the past is the focus on providing ways for the communities to sustain themselves. The next generation of African conservation managers must be equipped with the best training available. CCF's objectives are to develop programs that will empower Africans to manage their land and wildlife in an economically-sound and sustainable manner.

Throughout Africa, luxury tourism lodges are being developed in many of the protected area landscapes. Responsibly-developed tourism, done in consultation with wildlife forums, conservancies, game reserves, and NGO's, can promote economic development to rural areas. Small, low-impact lodges that are built in an eco-friendly way tell the story of African conservation. Capacity building empowers local communities to make money from crafts, employment at lodges, and other eco-tourism activities.

In addition to the development of tourism related jobs (e.g. tour guides, arts and crafts manufacturers, and other entrepreneurs), investment in local people promotes sustainable livestock farming practices that reduce the effects of habitat fragmentation. Successful examples of local conservancies and trans-boundary land management planning are providing a basis for developing large-scale land management plans for the future. These are Cheetahscapes.

Cheetahs are one
of the biggest
highlights for
international
tourists visiting
Africa.

184

Bushblok – Restoring the Cheetah's Habitat

CCF Bush Pty. Ltd is one of the practical solutions to benefit cheetah and humans. CCF's Bush project has helped develop a new forest industry in Namibia through selectively harvesting hundreds of square miles of thickened thornbush annually, while creating a new semi-skilled job opportunity for local people. From the harvested bush biomass, CCF Bush produces Bushblok, an award-winning, low-emission, high-heat fuel log certified by the Forest Stewardship Council™ (FSC).[28] CCF Bush monitors the harvested areas for biodiversity thereby restoring the cheetah's habitat. Our research has shown that there is a 25-tons-per-acre selective harvest yield from the bush. While bush encroachment is considered a major problem in Namibia, it also has potential as a renewable resource for alternative energy, especially in rural areas, and to alleviate electricity shortages projected to affect the country in the near future. CCF Bush is developing opportunities not only to restore and increase cheetah habitat, but to address two of Namibia's and Africa's biggest issues: electrification and poverty. Namibia currently faces a 50 percent unemployment rate. By expanding CCF Bush Pty Ltd, its harvesting of thornbush and processing efforts to make fuel could fire power plants and significantly reduce Namibia's power deficit, while providing employment to hundreds of Namibians.

The CCF Bush project encourages habitat restoration and the creation of a viable market for biomass products harvested in an environmentally and socially appropriate way.

It is a standout program that demonstrates that communities do not have to choose between economic development and wildlife conservation in order to thrive. In 2008, CCF's innovation with Bushblok was recognized with the awarding of the Tech Museum's Intel Prize for the Environment, and, in 2010, I was awarded the Tyler Prize for Environmental Achievement.

Eco-labels allow consumers' choices to promote conservation and sustainability.

The survival of the cheetah is in the hands of farmers. Since CCF is located in the heart of Namibia's farmland, where a third of the world's cheetah population occurs, we see a responsibility in both saving the cheetah and improving the lives and livelihoods of the farmers: our neighbors.

Eco-labels are seals or logos indicating that a product meets a set of meaningful and consistent standards for environmental protection and/or social justice. Increasingly, today's consumers are looking for eco-labels to help guide their purchases and are willing to pay extra for products that are healthy and good for the environment. This purchase power can steer businesses into adopting appropriate environmental standards.

Eco-labels also give producers a venue to tell their unique story and highlight their product in the market. Cheetah Country™ is a brand developed and trade marked by CCF for predator-friendly products from cheetah-range countries and is helping to support cheetah conservation. With this brand, CCF hopes to transform the cheetah from "vermin," or a threat to farmers' livelihoods, to an icon of speed and grace, an important part of the ecosystem, and a wildlife treasure that can foster tourism and economic development.

CHEETAH COUNTRY BEEF
free-range predator friendly farming

Currently most of the world's farmers do not see an economic benefit in having cheetah and other predators on their land. To many, the ecological value of predators does not outweigh the potential losses that predators cause. The Cheetah Country Beef certification program hopes to turn this around.

Cheetah Country Beef is an eco-label developed for cattle farmers who use predator-friendly farming practices. Interested farmers will sign an agreement saying they will not indiscriminately kill cheetahs on their farmland. In return for their efforts of implementing predator-friendly management practices they receive a premium price per pound of meat sold.

A PRODUCT OF CHEETAH COUNTRY

The premium paid to Cheetah Country Beef farmers is not intended to act as a compensation scheme. The premium is intended to help farmers implement non-lethal predator control measures such as calving kraals and the use of guarding animals. CCF believes that its predator friendly eco-labeling scheme can be adapted and used to save all the world's predators.

CCF's Model Farm covers over 100,000 acres of integrated livestock and wildlife farmland where our livestock is also used in our Future Farmers of Africa training programs. CCF's farm businesses help support its continued research, conservation, and education programs. One aspect of this research is the development of sustainable business models to teach value-added benefits to small stock farmers, and includes its Dancing Goat Creamery. All of CCF's creamery's products use milk from its Saanen and French Alpine dairy goats, which are farmed under the protection of CCF's celebrated Livestock Guarding Dogs.

The creamery makes goat milk products including cheeses, fudge, and ice cream and is part of CCF's mission to conserve wild cheetah. CCF's Model Farm is looking at economic alternatives once the thornbush is harvested, and growing grapes is a potential diversified livelihood for farmers. By creating these kinds of small enterprises, CCF is training appropriate skills to rural community members and to students of agriculture and food sciences making these products, while also showing farmers how to create supplemental income streams that complement their small livestock farming.[29]

CCF is a co-founder of the Wildlife Friendly Enterprise Network (WFEN) to promote wildlife conservation through facilitation and certification of responsible production practices, enterprise development, education, and branding. Both CCF's Bushblok™ and Dancing Goat Creamery products now feature a specially-designed label indicating that they have met WFEN's standards for certification.

Our goal is to expand the marketplace for producers that not only offer quality products but hope for the future for the world's most threatened species and the communities that live alongside them.[30]

CCF's Ambassador, Chewbaaka

When I first met Chewbaaka he was only 10 days old, starved and close to death. I bottle fed him and raised him by hand. Chewbaaka then spent the next 16 years of his life as our educational ambassador, by my side, as I worked with Namibian farmers, school children and youth, and international biologists and conservationists. Chewbaaka is a legend in Namibia and the inspiration to hundreds of thousands of people who met him in person or through his multiple "star" roles on wildlife documentaries, and most importantly, he was an icon and voice of all the remaining wild cheetahs in the world.

Those who met him will never forget him. Chewbaaka became a tangible symbol of CCF's vision of a world where humans and cheetahs could thrive together, in the wild, not as tame pets. However, those which have been orphaned, like he was or those that will never be able to live in the wild, are usually raised as educational ambassadors so that people everywhere know what this amazing species looks like, how it walks, purrs, chirps, and runs.

We can learn from cheetah ambassadors that we need a gentler world: one that will provide recourse for this non-aggressive, savanna hunter, whose females care gently for their young cubs, raising them while helping to provide for the rest of the veld's predators. Growing up, Chewbaaka would go with me to check camera traps I had placed at playtrees; he continued to go into the bush with me the rest of his life allowing humans

to follow him as he climbed into playtrees and left his mark. I learned so much from Chewbaaka and am honored that I had the opportunity to raise him and share him with so many people from around the world, all who considered him an inspiration. His gentle demeanor helped people understand why CCF is working so hard to save his wild cousins. In honor of his passing in 2011, CCF created a legacy giving program to honor individuals who establish a legacy gift to CCF in their will or charitable trust with a membership in the Chewbaaka Society. The cheetah's survival is in our hands and we can reach this goal in our lifetime to save the cheetah from extinction. Please join us.

Growing a Conservation Army

CCF's training and capacity-building efforts are aimed at helping build Namibia's institutional capacity as well as educate conservation students from throughout the world. Specific training includes conservation biology, natural resource management, appropriate land use, and livestock and wildlife management. Over 300,000 Namibian students, youth, farmers, and other stakeholders have participated in CCF's education programs in the past 20 years.

Our youth are our future. Students will soon take on roles as the teachers, wildlife managers or farmers of the future.

The Orphan Calf and the Magical Cheetah

Cheetah poems, essays and illustrations by children of Namibia

Cheetah Conservation Fund

In Namibia, CCF's educational programs expose over 20,000 learners every year to the research and conservation tools we have developed for managing the farmland ecosystem. Our Educational Outreach vehicle is on the road regularly, taking the message "We Can Live Together" to schools and communities. In addition, CCF's International Field Research and Education Center has been called the "best, most comprehensive cheetah educational museum in the world." The Center allows school learners to participate in nature trails and game drives. CCF also creates and disseminates education materials worldwide.[31]

The Orphan Calf and the Magical Cheetah is the result of an art and writing competition in Namibia to give school learners an opportunity to express their appreciation of the natural environment and the role of predators in the ecological balance of our natural world. From fanciful tales of how the cheetah got its spots to more realistic depictions of cheetahs falling prey to poachers or cubs being orphaned because their mother was shot or caught in a trap, by expressing themselves the children broadened their own perspectives regarding the dilemma facing the cheetah and commit themselves to promote its future survival.

Namibia's Founding President, His Excellency Dr. Sam Nujoma, is the Cheetah Conservation Fund's International Patron. He has been instrumental in helping his ministers and regional government officials, in particular tourism officers, to embrace CCF's message, "We Can Live Together." The Namibian model of education has proven very effective. Farmers that once saw cheetahs as nothing but vermin, now participate in conserving them and understand the role of the cheetah and other predators in healthy ecosystems. Communities that turned a blind eye to the slaughter of hundreds of cheetahs a year now celebrate Namibia's identity as the "Cheetah Capital of the World."

Cheetahs are a model for conservation of predators throughout the world.

Carnivores are important indicators of functioning ecosystems and, through predation, impact all aspects of the system. However, large carnivore populations are declining globally, with 22 of 30 large carnivore species considered endangered and all subject to a multitude of pressures including habitat degradation, conflict with agriculture, hunting, disease, and commercial trade. Of the carnivores, all the 37 species of Felidae (big and small cats) are either classified as threatened or endangered, except for the domestic cat.

Through their evolutionary history, carnivores have helped shape the evolution of their prey by hunting selection, which has provoked the development of fitness-enhancing anti-predator strategies. In addition, carnivores have influenced human evolution by enhancing our senses against predation and we may in part owe the evolution of our large brain and reasoning abilities to carnivores. Through scavenging predator kills for themselves, early hominids were provided a high-quality food source that may have enabled them to emerge from Africa and inhabit the globe.

CCF has become a model for carnivore conservation worldwide. Lessons learned from cheetah research and conservation efforts have taught us that humans can live with cheetahs and other predators through appropriate livestock and land-use management strategies. Humans and wildlife can live together.

CCF has used the results of its scientific research as the foundation for a variety of conservation and education programs that integrate human needs with cheetah management. Over the years, we have helped establish collaborative programs in Kenya, Botswana, Zimbabwe, South Africa, and Iran (where the last pocket of Asiatic cheetahs lives), while assisting research and training in countries such as Algeria, Benin, Ethiopia, Mozambique, Niger, and Zambia. However, there is an urgent need to accelerate the implementation of CCF's programs across cheetah range countries.[32] Future farmers must be taught and encouraged to practice management that tolerates predators through restored habitat and rangeland management. The farmers need to learn to sustainably grow grasses leading to healthy management of both livestock and wild game populations. The reduction in both game fencing and the stocking of non-native game species in game farms needs to be encouraged through the establishment of conservancies allowing for movement of wildlife through the landscape.

CCF has been a leader in the Conservancy initiative and is an active member in the Waterberg Conservancy. CCF's "own backyard" is the Greater Waterberg Landscape: an area of nearly four million acres which includes the Waterberg Conservancy, the Waterberg National Park, and four rural Conservancies in the Eastern communal areas known as Hereroland. Through collaboration, both within protected areas and on private lands, it should be possible to maintain large, intact ecosystems for the cheetah, which is the most critical aspect of future conservation both for cheetahs and for other large carnivores.[33]

With the cheetah populations dwindling through most other range countries, the cheetah's survival depends on educated people using proven methods to reverse this trend. Since 1990, CCF has developed, promoted, or adopted many programs that reduce conflict with the cheetah and is now sharing this information and providing training for wildlife conservation professionals internationally.[34] CCF has become a model conservation program recognized globally.

The Cheetahs' Future

The need to conserve the cheetah does not come into the mind of most rural Africans who have lost livestock or game through cheetah predation. The farmers' interests are in economic gain, be it through the sale of livestock, selling game as trophies to foreign hunters, or through eco-tourism. This is the harsh reality for the cheetah today in many areas of Africa and in particular southern Africa and Namibia, its last major refuge. Can the economic needs of the people be provided for while at the same time meeting the biological and ecological requirements of the cheetah?[35]

In the framework of the current environ-mental crisis, conservationists, government and businesses should work globally to develop big solutions to the world's big problems. Humans have both a spiritual and physical need for nature, but today's nature is out of balance. As human land-use has the greatest impact on the distribu-tion and abundance of cheetahs, monitoring several parameters, including population frag-mentation, health, and habitat loss, is necessary so as to not miss important elements, which may affect species survival.

The "Face of Africa" needs trained and dedicated people. As human populations continue to rise, agriculture claims more and more land, leading to more human/livestock-wildlife conflicts.

Overall, through collaborative research and multi-disciplined approaches, both within protected areas and on private lands, it can be possible to maintain large, intact ecosystems for the cheetah, which is the most critical aspect of future conservation, not just for cheetahs but also for other large carnivores. Cheetahs survival today is in the hands of humans and although research can provide solutions through knowledge gained, cheetah conservation needs awareness in sustainable land use for accommodating livestock and game farming activities in harmony with habitat, prey species, and predators, and the global public to help implement them.

Conclusion

Despite all the problems facing the cheetah, including their genetic uniformity, competition with other large carnivores, and human wildlife conflict, this magnificent animal, one of the oldest Felid species, has survived thousands of years. These icons of speed and grace continue to fill their ecological role as the world's fastest mammalian top predator. Integrated conservation programs across large landscapes will assure the survival of the cheetah for future generations.

"At the current pace, the cheetah is not going to live into too many more generations. We as people can do something. The animals can't do it. They are in our hands. They are stuck. Are we going to start marking on the calendar the days on earth that we are going to see cheetahs? That's where we are right now. Our children's children won't be able to see this animal on earth. They are going to look at a picture book and they are going to say, 'Did you live at that time and why didn't you do anything?' "

Dr. Laurie Marker

Appendix

Research, Genetics and The Future

Evolutionary History
1, pg. 82
An evolutionary history of the cheetah and other modern felid species has been constructed by paleontologists from fossils and, more recently, by geneticists using DNA. Present records date carnivores to the Eocene epoch, about 50 million years ago, with the specialized family Felidae evolving in the Miocene about 20 million years ago.

Dating the Genetic Bottleneck
2, pg. 83
Microsatellite variation growth depends on individual mutation rates, yet we can use average mutation rates to estimate how long it has been since the population bottleneck reduced variation in the protein coding gene region. According to Dr. O'Brien, the estimated time elapsed using this approach ranges from 488 to 1786 generations or a minimum of between 2,928 and 10,716 years to generate the present microsatellite variation in cheetahs. Today, the cheetah microsatellite variation shows a pattern of a recently and ongoing expanding population.

Our early genetic research was measured by allozymes variation in the Major Histocompatibility Complex (MHC-RFLP) and skin fibroblast proteins. One of the most extreme examples of the lack of genetic diversity was shown when cheetahs failed to reject skin allographs from unrelated cheetah donors at a landmark MHC study at the Wildlife Safari cheetah breeding center in Oregon that I managed in 1982. The cheetahs reacted as if they were immunological clones or identical twins. The bottleneck and associated loss of genetic variation has also been linked to several important life history characteristics of cheetahs including increased fluctuating asymmetry in metric skull measurement, relatively low levels of normal spermatozoa in males, immunologically accepted reciprocal skin grafts between unrelated individuals, and an increased susceptibility to infectious disease agents.

Cheetah Sub-species
3, pg. 88
Seven cheetah subspecies have been recognized and are *Acinonyx jubatus venaticus* (Asia and North Africa) (Griffith 1821), *Acinonyx jubatus hecki* (north-west Africa) (Hilzheimer 1913), *Acinonyx jubatus soemmeringii* (North Africa) (Fitzinger 1855), *Acinonyx jubatus raineyii* (*Acinonyx jubatus velox* has been included with *A.j. raineyii*) (East Africa) (Heller 1913), *Acinonyx jubatus jubatus* (southern Africa) (Schreber 1776) and the now extinct *Acinonyx jubatus raddei* (Turkestan), probably similar to *A.j. venaticus* (Hilzheimer 1913), however five subspecies are currently considered. Research has allowed us to better understand the genetic distance between the subspecies, which are closely related to each other.

CCF's Standardized Biological Sampling Methodologies
4, pg. 91
CCF has developed standardized sampling methodologies to assist researchers in other cheetah-range countries to safely and effectively develop similar programs and comparable data.

Disease, Surveillance, and Research
5, pg. 91
Captive populations of cheetah worldwide are known to have a high prevalence of rare diseases, unusual degenerative diseases, and elaborate inflammatory responses to common infections, compounded by chronic stress. The character of these diseases implicate stress as an important underlying factor, as well as a genetic predisposition and diet as possible confounding factors. CCF's non-releasable cheetahs have provided baseline data for long-term studies, as they are living in large enclosures within a natural environment considered stress free. CCF monitors fecal cortisol levels in relation to effects of stress on captive and wild cheetahs by collecting scat and extracting hormones from the samples. Gastric biopsies have been analyzed to better understand gastritis and how it affects captive animals over time. Investigations study individual cheetah behavioral profiles that are more likely to show high levels of corticoids and poor immune function and identify how this might be correlated with management risk factors and the development of disease.

6, pg. 92
Several diseases have been major health concerns in captive cheetahs after epidemics with high mortality occurred including Feline Infectious Peritonitis (FCoV/FIP). Efforts to control the disease have impacted captive management and breeding programs through reduced animal movements between institutions.

Census Techniques
7, pg. 93
By understanding the range and movements of the cheetah, farmers can reduce livestock-predator conflict. Namibian cheetahs have very large home ranges and often cover over 20 miles in two to three days.

8, pg. 93
CCF uses camera-traps to determine cheetah density. The cheetah triggers self-activating cameras and take their own pictures. Cheetahs' individual spot patterns allow for identification by CCF biologists. Using camera traps in conjunction with scat-detection dogs allows us to determine densities and movement, behavior, feeding patterns, and preferences of the censused cheetahs. Through the use of camera-trapping, capture histories can be built that estimate capture probabilities and thereafter, estimate cheetah numbers and densities using powerful capture-recapture models.

9, pg. 93
Habitat and dietary preferences, gender and social interactions, as well as the physiological health and reproductive productivity provide additional components to understanding cheetahs through on-going research. These data are critical for setting conservation priorities for cheetah throughout their range countries. Quantitative data, identifying and addressing threats to

the long-term survival of the cheetah is imperative. Only with the knowledge acquired through research is it possible to influence national policy in favor of cheetah conservation, identify conservation priorities for cheetah, or assess the effectiveness of management action.

Given the secretive nature of cheetahs, indirect census techniques are likely to be the only viable method of collecting useful population information. Indirect censusing relies upon the detection of signs such as spoor or scat and has been used effectively to gain population data for a wide range of species. However, census techniques have been limited by the ability of human searchers to find signs (a particular problem in Namibia's thick thorn bush habitat) and might result in incorrect species identification after signs are located. Detection or search dogs have proven to be a valuable tool and have demonstrated nearly 100 percent correct species identification record.

Genetics Lab
10, pg. 95
Due to the advances in genetic techniques over the past few decades, the acknowledgement of the role of genetics on wild species management and conservation efforts has resulted in an ever-increasing use of molecular tools. CCF realized the need for a genetic laboratory and the value of information that could be gained using molecular tools to aid with conservation and management. Applied Biosystems, now Life Technologies, provided a 310 genetic analyzer and all necessary support equipment and analytical software to establish the CCF's genetics laboratory in Namibia.

Does an animal in captivity represent the future?
11, pg. 96
More people visit zoos in the United States than attend all sports activities combined and represent a valuable link between their visitors and the conservation work they do in the field and allow people to learn and care about animals that inhabit faraway continents in habitats that they may never have the opportunity to see firsthand.

12, pg. 96
Several species have been saved from extinction through captive breeding programs.

Years of research on the cheetah both in situ and ex situ have provided extensive knowledge on genetics, reproduction, disease and behavior, and working with people in their range countries is critical for species survival.

International Cheetah Studbook
13, pg. 97
The number of breeding animals and the effective population size (Ne) of the captive cheetah population worldwide have increased, with Ne reaching 273.3, or 16.5 percent of the total population, in 2012. In comparison, the effective population size from 1988, the year of the first International Cheetah Studbook, was 111.4, or 11.9 percent of the captive population, showing an increase in 25 years.

The U.S. Cheetah SSP places breeding animals in regional breeding centers around the country where valuable breeding animals can be held off-exhibit. The facilities are large, reducing stress and providing a larger number of animals

for mate choice to increase the number of possible breeding pairs and ensure diversified bloodlines.

Applied Reproductive Techniques
14, pg. 98
Considering the threatened status of the cheetah and the difficulty in collecting samples, CCF's sample collection represents a treasure trove of information that can be used to save the cheetah. In cooperation with NZP researchers, CCF collects sperm from its orphan male cheetahs, which has been used in a Glycerol Toxicity Cryopreservation Study to develop more successful freeze-thaw methodologies for the cheetah.

CCF Sanctuary
15, pg. 99
Every effort is made to care for the animal's health at the CCF veterinary clinic; and in the case of an adult cheetah, to reintroduce it to the wild as soon as practical. Only those animals that are too young or not healthy enough to be released remain under the care of CCF's animal experts.

Africa: Romancing the Reality

Human Population Growth
16, pg. 113
As the human population grows, wildlife and the natural world pay the price as wildlife habitat is developed, air and water are polluted, and the climate crisis deepens. The world population, currently at 7.2 billion people, is predicted to increase by nearly another one billion people by 2025. With more than 200,000 people added to the planet every day, the population will further increase to 9.6 billion by 2050. Africa's population continues to grow constraining efforts to address poverty, create jobs, and protect the environment.

Climate Change
17, pg. 113
According to Namibia's Ministry of Environment and Tourism in the next 40 years Namibia's summer temperatures are predicted to become between 1.8° F and 6.3° F warmer and between 1.8° F and 7.2° F warmer in the winter. Over the past 40 years, more days exceed 95° F and fewer days are below 41° F. This change can affect the reproductive success of wildlife and also affect disease as a result of environmental stress. Species would naturally adapt to these fluctuating climatic conditions by engaging in local migration. For this to occur, it will be necessary to identify and develop migratory corridors.

Tourism - The Safari Code: sharing what is acceptable and not while on safari.
18, pg. 126
Drivers and guides should be trained not to approach predators, supported by a predator-friendly rating system with incentives and certifications, providing reputable operators with a marketing advantage they do not currently have. Parks could provide discounts to certified safari companies encouraging them to employ better drivers.

Education on good safari ethics is needed to help travelers gain an enlightened view of responsible tourism that could help the cheetah. Governments and tourism businesses need to help ensure that tourists and tour operators are aware of the safari ethics by distributing of pamphlets, posters, and education materials. Wildlife filmmakers should make a point of educating viewers to deter them from trying to imitate them when on a safari. Cheetah One is a 911 solution. It is an anti-harassment vehicle established in the Masai Mara to supervise tourist behavior around cheetahs and enforce park rules.

Game-fenced Farms
19, pg. 141
To mitigate economic losses, game farmers could erect electric fencing in selected sections of farms to manage these more expensive game animals or use swing gates (wildlife "doggie" doors) that keep cheetahs out of these select areas but allow other game movement. These initiatives should be a part of a game farm management plan, linked to permitting regulations as a part of government policy, as most game fenced areas are not conservation areas but private businesses. Proposed game laws in Namibia stipulate that game-fenced areas cannot eliminate wildlife indiscriminately for private gain. However, game farmers continue to catch and kill more cheetahs than livestock farmers.

Illegal Trade
20, pg. 143
The illegal trade in plant and animal products, such as ivory, rhino horns, and skins, has been one of the greatest pressures on wild species. Since the early 1970s, trade restrictions through CITES have been implemented at a global level as a tool to control trade and thus conserve wild populations. Implementation of regulations has had varied levels of success.

21, pg. 154
Despite international laws and government bans on importing big cats for pets, illegal traders are smuggling these animals, which is known as an "open secret" among residents. The governments are working on tougher laws against the illegal animal trade and more cheetah awareness campaigns.

22, pg. 155
Although our main network is in northern Africa, we have received reports of a smaller number of cheetahs illegally traded from Angola, Tanzania, Kenya, South Africa, Cameroon, Zambia, Zimbabwe, and Botswana. In Namibia, 15 cheetahs were confiscated from one owner by the Ministry of Environment and Tourism under suspicion that the cheetahs were destined for illegal trade or hunting. All cats were moved to the CCFs sanctuary.

23, pg. 155
CCF's staff regularly meet with officials from the US and other nations including Ethiopia and the United Arab Emirates (UAE) to advocate for the end of the illegal pet trade in cheetahs. CCF's data documenting the number of cases, particularly from the Horn of Africa and the Middle East, has contributed to United States and international efforts to combat illegal wildlife trade, including the 2013 CITES Conference of the Parties in Bangkok where, for the first time, the illegal pet trade in cheetahs was listed as an agenda item.

Changing the "Face of Africa"
Livestock Guarding Dogs
24 pg. 164
Despite reaching full height by around 12 months of age, Anatolian and Kangal dogs mature slowly reaching behavioral maturity only at 18-30 months old. Protectiveness reaches a peak at three to four years of age when they reach their true potential as an effective guardian. CCF has helped establish livestock guarding dog programs in several other countries including South Africa and Tanzania. CCF's methods of training livestock guarding dogs and farmers have been used as models elsewhere in the world to protect other predators such as mountain lions, jaguars, and wolves.

Future Farmers of Africa
25, pg. 166
CCF has hosted a few thousand livestock farmers for week-long courses that teach everything from basic mechanics to non-lethal predator control to help increase the health of their livestock and give them tools for preventing predation on their animals. Farmers are taught livestock and wildlife management techniques and simple solutions like bringing the cows closer to the homestead before calving: integrating donkeys into the herds as fierce protectors of the livestock, and using livestock guarding dogs.

26, pg. 169
The cheetah's survival requires sound farmland and prey species management, and habitat stability. Ecological monitoring of game species through game counts and training of community game guards is important. CCF has trained over 300 cheetah-range country biologists at CCF's Center in Namibia.

Rehabilitation and Reintroduction of Cheetah Back into the Wild
27, pg. 173
Rehabilitation is the process of training and release of a species into the wild most often from a captive sanctuary to other areas as an option if the species is endangered or extinct in the wild. It can only be successful in areas that can support adequate prey populations and reduced human, livestock, and wildlife conflict.

India's last cheetahs were exterminated in the 1940s. In 2007, a courageous and determined effort by conservation-minded citizens of India was launched to explore the restoration of cheetahs into suitable habitat in their country. Spearheaded by noted Indian conservationists, Dr. M. K. Ranjitsinh and Dr. Divyabhanusinh Chavda, a workshop to plan and facilitate the reintroduction of cheetah to suitable habitats of their former range in India was convened in 2010 at Gajner, Rajasthan, home to a wildlife sanctuary where the last Indian cheetah survived. The workshop was attended by Indian conservation managers and scientists, Nature Reserve superintendents, and cheetah researchers, including CCF. CCF plays an advisory role and I have returned to India to consult. In order to have long-term success in reintroductions, cooperation within all of the cheetahs-range countries will be necessary and must be conducted under international guidelines.

Cheetahscapes

Bushblok – Habitat Restoration
28, pg. 185

The CCF's Bushblok factory molds this biomass refuse into eco-friendly fire log. It was opened in 2005 in Otjiwarongo with the help of United States Agency for International Development (USAID) and employs over 30 people. Thousands of tons of Bushblok have been distributed as an alternative to firewood and charcoal, and is sold in Namibia, South Africa, and the United Kingdom. CCF continues to promote the prospect of manufacturing pellets as a source of biomass for countries in Europe that are required to produce a percentage of their electricity using biomass. CCF's habitat research continues and studies have shown that areas that have been thinned, not clear-cut, quickly repopulate with wildlife, including cheetahs.

Cheetah Country Beef
29, pg. 187

Once the beef is introduced and consumers realize there is a way to contribute to cheetah survival by simply purchasing specialty beef the product's demand will grow. There is no limit to the number of farmers certified by this program. Ideally, all Namibian farmers will one day work together to save the wildlife, predators, and the environment with which they live and be supported for this through consumer price premiums on the meat.

In 2013, CCF helped launch the Namibian Wine Growers Association. Grapes grow in most soil types and have very deep roots similar to the thorn bushes that have encroached Namibia's farmlands. A few acres of wine grapes can provide an alternative to rural communities while other land can be used for integrated livestock and wildlife conservation sustainably.

Wildlife Friendly – An Eco-label
30, pg. 187

In 2007, at the Summit on Wildlife Friendly Enterprise, representatives from eight countries formalized the Wildlife Friendly Enterprise Network (WFEN). This non-profit organization has developed the Certified Wildlife Friendly® label that is setting the global standard for wildlife friendly enterprises while educating consumers on products that support good conservation. Certified Wildlife Friendly® develops, certifies, and promotes products and practices that conserve threatened wildlife while contributing to the economic vitality of rural communities. CCF has helped the Wildlife Friendly eco-label gain traction and encourages other predator organizations into this scheme

Education
31, pg. 194

CCF's school and youth education programs have been adapted by cheetah conservation organizations in other countries such as South Africa, Botswana, Kenya, Zimbabwe, Algeria, and Iran. As part of a global plan to save the cheetah for future generations, CCF uses its Namibian model to impart international education programs that illustrate ways in which the species can be protected.

Cheetah Range Country Plans
32, pg. 197

Over the past several years, working together with researchers and specialists, under the guidance of the IUCN Cat Specialist group and the Range Wide Planning for Cheetahs and Wild Dogs, meetings have taken place where regional and national plans have been designed. CCF has played a major role in these meetings and implementation of the plans.

Conservancies
33, pg. 197

Namibia's conservancy movement focuses on the benefits of natural resource management, attaching economic and cultural values to these resources while raising awareness of ecological issues. Educating the world about the value of both consumptive and non-consumptive use empowers local people so that they can be instrumental in responsible decision-making. The Greater Waterberg Landscape is a big model for the future. Plans include creating a landscape that will incorporate wildlife, livestock, and economic development through habitat restoration and ecotourism promoting cheetahs and wild dogs.

Conservation Strategy
34, pg. 197

Cheetah conservation is interconnected to social, economic, and environmental factors, which are of concern throughout the nations of Sub-Saharan Africa. The coming generation of African conservation managers must be equipped with the best training available to empower them to protect their land and wildlife in an economically sound manner. Growing existing programs that train land managers in the environmental value of appropriate range management, which optimizes the economic value of a sustainable, mixed wildlife-livestock system designed to avoid land degradation is necessary and needs partnerships and funding.

CCF's three-pronged strategy includes long-term studies to understand and monitor the factors affecting the cheetah's survival. Results are then used to develop conservation policies and programs to sustain cheetah populations and to work with local, national, and international communities to raise awareness, educate, and build capacity. Capacity building opportunities for local communities throughout the cheetahs' range must be encouraged, with the primary goal of showing how the linkage of sustainable practices provide direct and indirect benefits to communities.

The Future
35, pg. 199

Conservancies can fulfill both cheetah and human needs and can continue to maintain the necessary habitat for long-term cheetah conservation. From a scientific standpoint, insights gained from our research also provide ideas for conservation applications and lessons learnt in Namibia will be applicable to cheetahs and other predators facing similar conflict elsewhere

Cheetah Conservation Partners

Cheetah Conservation Fund
PO Box 2496
Alexandria, VA 22301-0496 USA
www.cheetah.org

Cheetah Conservation Fund
PO Box 1755
Otjiwarongo, Namibia
www.cheetah.org

Action For Cheetahs in Kenya (ACK)
PO Box 1611
00606 Nairobi, Kenya
www.actionforcheetahs.org

Cheetah Conservation Botswana
Mokolodi Nature Reserve
Private Bag 0457,
Gaborone, Botswana
www.cheetahbotswana.com

Cheetah Outreach
Firgrove Rural
Cape Town 7110, South Africa
www.cheetah.co.za

Iranian Cheetah Society (ICS)
PO Box 14155-8549
Tehran, Iran
www.wildlife.ir

Conservation of Asiatic Cheetah Project (CACP)
Office of the Conservation of the
Asiatic Cheetah Project
Pardisan Eco Park, Tehran, Iran
www.cacp.ir

Conservation Planning for Cheetah and African Wild Dog
www.cheetahandwilddog.org

Ruaha Carnivore Project
University of Oxford, Department of
Zoology
www.ruahacarnivorproject.com

Endangered Wildlife Trust (EWT)
Private Bag X11, Modderfontein, 1609
Johannesburg, South Africa
www.ewt.org.za

Large Carnivore Management Association of Namibia
www.carnivore-namibia.org

National Geographic, Big Cats
Initiative
1145 17th Street NW
Washington, D.C. 20090-8199, USA
www.animals.nationalgeographic.com/
animals/big-cats-initiative

Panthera
8 West 40th Street, 18th Floor
New York, NY 10018, USA
www.panthera.org

IUCN Cat Specialist Group
Thunstrasse 31
Muri b. Ber 3074, Switzerland
www.catsg.org

Smithsonian Institution's National Zoo and Conservation Biology Institute
www.nationalzoo.si.edu/SCBI

Wildlife Conservation Network
25745 Bassett Lane
Los Altos, CA 94022, USA
www.wildnet.org

Certified Wildlife Friendly
www.wildlifefriendly.org

Coalition Against Wildlife Trafficking
www.CAWTglobal.org

International Conservation Caucus Foundation
www.ICCFoundation.US